Inspire.

DEVOTIONS FOR BUSY YOUNG PEOPLE

PAUL MARTIN

Inspire – Devotions for busy young people Unlocking Revelation – © 2020 Paul Martin

Other books by this author:
Inspire. A resource for busy youth workers. Volumes 1 & 2.
Inspire. Devotions for busy youngsters. Psalm 34 - A recipe for faith.
Inspire. Devotions for busy youngsters. Psalm 139 – Finding identity.

www.inspiredevotions.com

Illustrations by Paul Martin.

Cover design Oliver Pengelli

Artwork for Inspire light bulb adapted and modified from an original line drawing by Amy Walters (www.amywaltersdesign.co.uk). Permission is granted solely for use by Paul Martin in his Inspire series and may not be replicated elsewhere.

To all you busy young people out there.
May you receive all of the good things
that God has in store for you!

Be inspired!

ACKNOWLEDGEMENTS

I would like to thank my wonderful wife Deb, my Sweetie. Thanks so much for the many sacrifices that you made over the past nine months, so that I could write this book! I could not have done this without your patience and understanding! Thank you for proof reading too! I love you lots!

Thanks to Alfie for all your thoughts on what is best for this book and your prayer space ideas. Your input has been brilliant! Thanks to both you and Henry for being patient with me in the many weeks of writing this book! You boys are wonderful and I love you three thousand.

Thank you Mum & Dad for your listening ears and wise words, through everything that goes on in my world! I hope I remember to tell you about the amazing things that happen too! Thanks so much for all your OXOs! Lol! I appreciate all the corrections that you've spotted and all your ideas as you have gone through the pages of this book. Much love to you both!

Thank you Simon Genoe for all of your encouragements! You are such an incredible communicator. It's privilege to learn from you.

Thank you Carlton Baxter for being a great support to me with my writing and checking out this book.

Thank you Richard Lyttle for the great photo that you took of me! Perfect for the back cover pic!

Thank you Oliver Pengilley for your original painting for the front cover.

Thank you Amy Walters for your light bulb line drawing, which has become the logo for my Inspire books. I love the prophetic insight that comes through your art and design work. You are truly gifted.

Thank you Evie MacDonald for your illustrations that have I've featured in one of my prayer spaces. You are a really creative artist!

And a big shout out to all my "yoof" at Magheralin Parish. I love yous lots!

ABOUT THIS BOOK

Take a look at the picture above. It's a sketch of a photograph that was taken at London Zoo.ᵃ When I first looked at the photo I couldn't work it out. "Why is this lion so close to the zoo keeper?" I wondered. "Is that not very dangerous?" Maybe it's a very tame lion" I thought. "But why is the zoo keeper placing down a two metre social distancing sticker on the floor? I'm not sure the lions will understand. Could they even contract the Corona virus?"

It was only until my son Alfie pointed out that there was a pane of glass in between the zoo keeper and the lion that I understood the picture! Reading the book of Revelation is a bit like this. At first it can appear to be a confusing picture that doesn't relate. However, once someone points out one or two important details to show you what you are looking at, suddenly it all makes sense! I really believe that God wants us to understand all of His words, and that if we desire to understand them; He will unlock its mysteries and reveal them to us. To have a book called "Revelation" and have it remain a mystery would be very ironic.

As I have read the book of Revelation, it has given me a fresh perspective on life. I have understood more about God and His Kingdom as well as gained a fresh a confidence about the future. It is a powerful book. I hope you enjoy reading Revelation as much as I have.

The way I've written this devotional book is a bit like a conversation between you, me and the Holy Spirit. Hopefully I'll be the one pointing out the panes of glass that are not immediately obvious, and the Holy Spirit will bring the power! Together we'll figure this thing out. Revelation 1:3 tells us, that as you read the words of Revelation you are going to be well blessed! So open your Bible and read that day's text from the book of Revelation before you read each devotion; then read the day's devotion to understand it more. It's probably going to be handy to re-read the Bible bits, because there's a lot in there to get to grips with.

Included in this devotional are prayer spaces for you to take all of your thoughts to Jesus. You can tell Him everything and I know He will put thoughts into your mind in return. Write it all down and you'll begin to figure out how Jesus talks to you.

I'd really like to pray for you at this point, as I sense God has some powerful things that He wants to say to you as you read on. Why not pray this prayer to God as you start these devotions...

Father God. I thank You for what I am about to read. Thank You that You have led me to this book. I ask that You would open my eyes to see what You want me to see. Reveal and inspire me deep within. Let me have a deeper understanding of You, of Your plans and Your ways, so that I will be moved to worship You like never before. In Jesus' name. Amen!

Contents

Contents

UNLOCKING REVELATION

Inspire.

DEVOTIONS FOR BUSY YOUNG PEOPLE

PAUL MARTIN

#Day1

A MESSAGE FROM JESUS

Revelation 1:1-3

Some time ago I had an intense dream... In the dream I was working as a government agent for the secret service MI5. As I walked down a dimly lit road, I observed some terrorist activity in preparation for an attack. I made it back to MI5 Head Quarters to report what I had seen. Immediate action was required, so as the field team got ready to intercept the terrorists, I also went to the weapons locker for a gun.

At this point my boss said to me that I wasn't going with the team, but had to look after the printer! This was not something I was keen on doing, as you can imagine, the printer was a lot less exciting. Reluctantly, I went over to the printer, to find it was out of paper. I filled it with paper and immediately it started up, printing out information, vital to the capture of the terrorists and essential to the team who had just left.

I then realised that although my role did not appear as exciting as that of the field team; however being responsible for getting the communications through to the rest of the team, was no less crucial to the mission.

This book of Revelation contains a message that comes directly from the Lord Jesus Christ Himself. It reveals to us further details about Jesus that aren't found in the Gospels. His words are recorded by John, who, much like the guy at the printer then passes this important information on to us. Reading Revelation is to be read as if Jesus is speaking directly to you and to me. John actually receives seven messages from God (otherwise known as visions), where the Lord communicates to him using the most vivid picture language of the things that must take place. The visions that John sees, tell us about the rule of God's Kingdom and how God's plans are unfolding. They also contain an insight into the very real spiritual battle that rages in the heavenlies. As God's children, you and I are involved.

We read the words in verse 3 *"Blessed is the one who reads aloud the words of this prophecy, and blessed are those who hear, and who keep what is written in it, for the time is near."* This book of Revelation was given to be read out loud to others, to be passed on so that others can also hear. So rather than being a mystery, God intends for all His people to get what it's about.

It would have been distributed amongst the followers of Jesus in Asia Minor; but what does it mean, *"the things that must soon take place"*? How can the word "soon" be relevant to those who first heard it read 2,000 years ago and yet also be relevant to us today? Revelation is still current because it contains events that are continuing to unfold. Some events in the book will have happened, and those things yet to take place may happen suddenly and unexpectedly. These insights are given to us beforehand so that we won't be afraid when world-shaking events develop at speed. Instead Jesus gives us an assurance that although we will live in challenging times, these are a necessary part of His purposes in the age we are living in. God's will still unfolds through troubled times. The *"time is near"* for certain tasks of His kingdom to be put into action in greater ways. As we read the words of this book, we get a vivid picture of what's going on in the spiritual realm as well as an insight into its direct effect on the world.

Jesus is the central figure of history. He hasn't finished saving this world, there is more to come. Don't be put off by the drama. The promise of this book is that you will receive God's blessings through reading it. It will also give you essential information into the unseen fight that affects you and me as we serve as God's agents on earth.

Lord Jesus, I thank you that it is your desire for me to understand what is written in the book of Revelation. I ask that You would reveal to me the truth of Your words through everything that I read. In your holy Name!

Lord I want to know more...

What is it You are telling me about Yourself today?

How do I fit into Your plan?

Lord, this is what I love about You...

How can I share this with others?

GOD'S REALM

Revelation 1:4-6

Have you ever watched a film that involves Super hero characters jumping from one reality or realm to another? In the Marvel Avengers comics, you'll find stories of heroes risking their lives by travelling through alternate realities, to locate beings with special powers from another dimension who are needed to save earth. In a world that has experienced disaster, Ant Man navigates a "Quantum realm" through time and space, to help reverse the devastation of an attack of epic proportions. Of course this is all science fiction, but more and more of what we're going to read in the book of Revelation, refers to real events that take place in another dimension, the heavenly realm.

The part we read today starts with the words, *"John to the seven churches that are in Asia: Grace and peace from Him who was and is and is to come, and from the seven spirits who are before His throne."* Here we see two realms referred to: our earthly realm, where the churches exist, and the heavenly realm of God's throne. Do you notice that God the Holy Spirit exists in both of these realms? He's present in the churches addressed here, as well as present in the throne room of heaven. Activity is taking place in heaven that directly impacts our reality on earth. Being in both realities, brings the power and activity of God to us in the here and now. When you feel God is close, or experience an answer to prayer, that is the Holy Spirit making it happen on earth. It's the Holy Spirit who proves to us of the reality of God. He also helps us to understand the necessary truth that we are separated from God because of our wrongs.

I expect you're wondering, "Why does it say *seven spirits*? I thought there was just one Holy Spirit?" What this is doing, is giving a description of the

Holy Spirit, by giving Him a name. It doesn't literally mean there is seven of Him, just like Jesus being "the lamb of God" doesn't make Him a sheep. The Holy Spirit is said to have seven attributes, so He is given seven different names to describe these features. An example of one name that refers to the Holy Spirit is the "Spirit of wisdom." Additionally, the number seven is intended to match up with the seven churches, indicating that the Holy Spirit is present in the seven churches.

The number seven in the Bible is quite significant. It communicates the idea of something or someone being complete, not lacking; it also means the whole of something. So there being seven churches will also represent the whole of the church throughout the earth in its different forms. You know, sometimes people see different denominations as being a divided company of people, but actually when added together, like pieces of a puzzle we make the whole picture.

Jesus is described as *"the faithful witness,"* the word used in the Greek you might be familiar with is "martyr." You will find Jesus in the historical documents of the writers at the time. The event of His crucifixion by the Romans is the saving event of mankind where *"He has freed us from our sins by His blood."* Jesus, God's Son came into the time and space of earth. His death and coming alive again connects us to the reality of heaven and God's kingdom. This is not an imaginary thing, but a powerful reality that we have access to, through His self-sacrifice. He paid for our lives with His blood, saving us from a judgement we deserve.

As you read on, you'll notice that some events take place as a result of judgements made by God. It's important that we take in the words found at the beginning of this letter, *"Grace and peace from Him..."* It's not God's desire to bring judgement and fear to His children, or even to this world. For those who don't know Him, He has made the ultimate sacrifice for all of us to respond and receive His undeserved favour and peace.

Lord Jesus. It is because You left heaven and gave up Your life for me, that what I say to You now, is heard in heaven. Please show me what Your offer of life and being made free from judgement really means.

The Holy Spirit is described as the sevenfold Spirit in Isaiah 11:2. These words help us to understand what the Holy Spirit is like. As you pray, invite Him into your room now.

1. Spirit of the Lord. Holy Spirit You are welcome in this place.

2. Knowledge. Please show me more of Jesus and the Father.

3. Understanding. Help me to see things as You see them.

4. Wisdom. Inspire me with Your thoughts.

5. Counsel. Guide me in my decision making.

6. Might. Please overcome where I am weak.

7. Fear of the Lord. I worship and adore you holy God.

#Day3
ALL ABOUT JESUS
Revelation 1:7-8

How do you feel about thunderstorms? I know some people aren't into them, as they can sound a bit like something is going to come crashing through the window at any moment. I actually like them. I like to stay up and watch the lightning in a thunderstorm, like a fireworks display. I remember when I was young being out at night, coming back from the beach and seeing lightning far in the distance, over the waters. You could see for miles across the sea. It was both scary being outside with the noise of distant thunder, but also exciting at the same time seeing the flashes of lightning from far away.

The bit we've just read talks about the moment when Jesus will return. Jesus told His disciples several times that He would die, come alive again and then return to earth at a later time He called *"the end of the age."* The words *"Behold, He is coming with the clouds,"* refer to this event of Jesus' return (it's also in Matt 24:30). I don't know if you've wondered, "How is it possible for everyone to be able to see Jesus at the same time? Is He going to be on the television or arrive by aeroplane?" To appear for all to see would have to be a supernatural event. Jesus describes what to expect in Matthew 24:27; *"For as lightning that comes from the east is visible even in the west, so will be the coming of the Son of Man."*

You know how you can ring up a friend during a thunderstorm? (Don't use a landline!). Even though you're in different houses, you can both look out of your window and see the same lightning. In the same way that two people can see the same lightning, from different locations; so we will all see Jesus return, not on a screen, but in the air. When Jesus went up into heaven, two angels appeared as the disciples stared skyward. The angels said to the disciples that Jesus *"will come back in the same way you have seen Him go into heaven"* (Acts 1:11). His appearance will be from the sky. I guess you can expect the weather report on that day to be cloudy!

There's a good reason why Jesus said that He will return in this way. It's so that we will know it's Him. In Jesus' times and since then, people have falsely claimed to be the Messiah, God's chosen One. Only the One who is truly God's Son will be able to appear in the sky for all to see. No human could say they were Jesus without making such a glorious return.

Jesus is the central figure not just of history, but of the future too. He is described as the Alpha and the Omega, which are the first and last letters of the Greek alphabet. This declares to us the truth that all things began with Him and all things will end with Him. It literally means "the One who has His hand on everything." Wow, what a powerful God!

Additionally the Bible tells us that we'll all witness this event, whether dead or alive. Those who were directly involved in His death will see Him and "wail on account of Him," realising who they actually killed. It's incredible, when we consider that Jesus, the Alpha and the Omega, allowed the religious leaders of the day, to hand Him over to the Romans to be executed by crucifixion. On His return, Jesus' death will be properly mourned by all who were responsible. For the friends of Jesus on that day, it would have been an unbelievably hard experience. Being unable to stop the soldiers as they brutally treated Jesus, and humiliated Him who only did good, knowing a terrible injustice was being carried out. The sorrow and pain must have been unbearable for this beautiful man who did no wrong.

Yet somehow, you and I are connected to this event. We find that it was our wrongs that held him on the cross until the work of His sacrifice was completed. Jesus, the King of glory, endured this execution willingly for us, to accomplish for us an eternity with Him, due to unfold at His return.

Lord Jesus. When I consider how you were literally a dead man walking as You carried that cross to Your execution for me, humiliated and alone. It is a moment to mourn. Thank you that You endured that for me. I love You.

I AM THE ALPHA
and the omega,
SAYS THE LORD GOD,
who is and who was and who
IS TO COME,
the almighty.

#Day4

ENDURING HARDSHIP

Revelation 1:9-11

Life under the rule of the Romans could be very precarious if you found yourself on the wrong side of the Empire. Imagine the Emperor has issued a decree: "Everyone must offer sacrifices to one of the Roman ancestral gods. Failure to do so will result in punishment." Unfortunately this is a problem for you. You are one of Jesus' disciples. In fact as His closest-friend, you were there on the days of His execution and resurrection. You cannot dishonour your devotion to Jesus by making a sacrifice in worship to a fake god. Yet the Romans will be on the lookout for any who do not comply! All conduct will be noted and monitored! Many of your friends have been executed, tortured or fed to the lions in Roman amphitheatres.

Then, the day comes. You are arrested. The accusations made are that political unrest is being stirred up under your leadership. So to make an example of you, your punishment will be torture. A bath of boiling oil is prepared for you. Yet something miraculous happens. Instead of being painful, it feels cool to the skin. The soldiers can't believe it. One of them tests it with his hand. It's hot!!! You are hauled out of the boiling pot unharmed and later sentenced to imprisonment by isolation, on the small Island of Patmos. Here you remain for some time, until one Easter Sunday, something happens, the Lord Jesus appears to you again.

According to the writer Tertullian, these are said to be the events that led up to the writing of the book of Revelation. At the time, Christians were facing daily persecution in the most difficult of circumstances. In the bit we just read, John writes about being *"a partner in the tribulation... on account of the word of God and the testimony of Jesus."* Alongside his fellow believers, John was also experiencing persecution for being a follower of Jesus, being targeted to suffer, simply because he was a Christian.

22

To be a Christian is to be like Christ. We know that Jesus was despised, suffered and was rejected and it is likely that as a Christian, you and I will experience persecution from others in some measure too. John calls himself a *"partner"* in *"the kingdom,"* meaning the Kingdom of God, which all Christians are a part of. We have access to the Lord God Almighty, like children in the house of a good and loving father. We'll know His immense blessings and favour, as we go through our lives, loving and serving Him; but there is also something else we share with the Lord. It's called *"the fellowship of His sufferings,"* in Philippians 3:10. When hardships come, but we keep going even though we're attacked for following Jesus, we are sharing in what He suffered for us. No one invites trouble, but when it comes because of the faith we have put in Him, we are proving our faith and partnering with Jesus.

So if you have suffered because you are a Christian and have been representing Jesus well, it shows that you are a true disciple of His. Jesus is sharing with you in your pain. So be encouraged. He is closer than you think! But here's a question... Why can't God just take away all the hardships? After all, He can do anything. Yes there will be a day for that. Read on and you'll find out more!

The book of Revelation was actually written for the followers of Jesus who were enduring incredible suffering, who were targeted because they were Christians. Throughout the book of Revelation God reveals more of what He's like, of the activity of heaven and also the things to come. This would have been of great encouragement to the persecuted church, as it was read aloud wherever it was sent. Maybe you've been wrongly treated, misunderstood or judged unfairly, because you are a Christian. It is not uncommon. Furthermore, in several countries today, people have been arrested simply for not denying their faith and worse still, others have been killed. God sees it all. He also sees the faithfulness of His people as something very, very precious.

Lord Jesus, help me to see the value of not giving up when things get tough. I know that You are with me and that when I suffer, You suffer too. Draw me close when I'm afraid and give me boldness to live for You.

Thank You for what You suffered for me

CONSIDER WHAT JESUS HAS DONE

Help me to understand what it cost You

WHAT DO YOU WANT TO TELL JESUS ABOUT?

Thank You that we can face tough times together

with You I can face anything

WHAT ARE YOU CONCERNED ABOUT FOR THE FUTURE?

#Day5

THE LIVING ONE

Revelation 1:12-20

What do you think about the idea of being immortal? Being able to live forever? Many a civilisation has aspired to the hope of discovering the secret to not growing old. What would you do, if you could live forever and not be killed? Might you aim for a life of luxury? Accumulating money to one day live the life of kings? Maybe you'd take up a dangerous job, such as a firefighter or in a bomb disposal unit, using your special powers to keep the vulnerable safe? Perhaps you'd be your own boss and become a vigilante like Batman, rescuing people who needed saving?

Then again, would you really want to be immortal and live on this earth forever? The last few decades have seen random acts of terrorism, accidents in nuclear facilities, as well as natural disasters all over the earth; making the future of life on this earth appear a lot more uncertain.

If any of this stuff worries you, Jesus has some reassuring words for you, *"Fear not, I am the first and the last, the living one. I died, and behold I am alive forevermore, and I have the keys of Death and Hades."* These words have come some 50 or so years after the event of Jesus' death, where Jesus talks about what He has won for us during those memorable days.

As John turned in response to the voice he heard, he saw the immortal Son of Man. Standing dressed in a fine robe, with the appearance of an Old Testament High Priest. As the go-between God and His people, a priest spoke on behalf of God, giving instruction and offering a yearly sacrifice to cancel out wrongs done. This person who stands before John identifies as the foremost priest there is, the actual Word of God who offered up His own life as the perfect sacrifice, so that we can be forgiven.

John takes a closer look to make out who the figure is, drawn to the striking colour of His hair, white like the wool of a pure lamb. In the book of Daniel 7:9, the Lord appears with white hair and is given the name *"the Ancient of days,"* signifying the everlasting God, older than the universe itself, with wisdom unmatched.

John begins to recognise this figure. It is Jesus. He gazes into the eyes of the Son of God to see they are blazing like a fire. John glimpses an intense aliveness, a holy purity, a genuine honesty and love, which searches the heart and knows what He sees. Who could hold the stare of Jesus? John turns his eyes away and looks to the floor, where he sees the feet of Jesus. They glow like the colour of bronze that has been through a furnace, showing that Jesus has been through a severe time of testing, enduring the torture of execution by the cross and proving His worth. The sound of Jesus' voice is powerful and majestic, as you would expect from a King. His words come like a weapon. When spoken, these are not just words of a past era. They are alive, speaking from God's throne into our day and time and active, striking with real power to cause events to change on the earth, defeating the power of the enemy.

Jesus confirms that He is indeed the immortal saving One; being the only one worthy to hold such power of immortality. The words "I am," come with the full meaning of the Old Testament name for God "I am who I am." In later times, this name of God (YHWH or Yahweh) was held in such respect that it was not spoken. He is the God that has always been, the immortal One; the only one deserving to hold the power of immortality. Leaving heaven, living as a man, being unjustly executed; His sacrificial death won authority to access Hades. Hades, the place of the dead, came under the devil's influence for those whose sins have not been atoned for. Jesus lived a completely sinless life; thus when Jesus died He was not under the devil's power. Taking back authority to access Hades, Jesus also beat death through His resurrection, gaining authority over death itself.

Jesus is the Living One. He reigns and rules over the universe. The events in this book are written, so that you will know that He has His hand on all things. He has won a prize for you, a reward that runs into eternity.

As you take some time to think on God, ask the Lord to highlight one or two of these phrases that He used to describe who He is.
Ask the Lord what He is telling you about Himself.

I am the bread of life (John 6:35-48)

I am the light of the world (John 8:12)

I am the gate (John 10:7)

I am the good shepherd (John 10:11-14)

I am the true vine (John 15:1-5)

I am the resurrection and the life (John 11:25)

29

#Day6

A LOST LOVE
Revelation 2:1-7

I expect you've had this experience: You've lost something important to you, such as a book, keys, or your phone. As you're searching around looking, it's normal to tell someone else what you're doing, since having more eyes on the task will cover greater ground. Those helping with your search will generally ask you either of the following questions, "Where did you have it last?" Or "Can you remember when you last used it?"

Often this seems like a pointless or irrelevant question, since you have probably already checked the places where you think you last used it. However, what the person is trying to do is to trigger pathways in your brain, plotting the course of events that lead you to discover why you lost that item in the first place. There it is, down the side of the sofa cushion!

We read today a letter, addressed to the angel of the church in Ephesus. As messengers, angels not only pass on communications to God's people in ways seen or unseen, but they also bring about God's interventions too. More than a message to just one church; this letter contains God's will for His people throughout all generations, world-wide. God's church is pictured as lampstands, like valuable gold furnishings fit for a king, reflecting the royalty of King Jesus and shining light in dark places.

Ephesus was a place dominated by a huge temple to a goddess called Artemis, listed by Antipater as one of the Seven Wonders of the World. All citizens were expected to show evidence of worship to this goddess. This was a problem for the Christians of the Ephesus. Thus at any time, followers of Jesus could be singled out by the Roman Empire, resulting in suffering and hardship. Additionally, some people had come to Ephesus as "leaders" and began teaching a kind of "pick and mix" approach to Christianity; with a bag of false religious ideas that weren't from God.

Belief is important. If truth is mixed with lies, it becomes worthless. So in an effort to keep true to the Gospel, the Church stood against any who taught false things about the Christian faith. This was a very good thing. It kept out a number of con artists who could have led many into confusion.

However, over the years, the focus of preserving the right and rejecting the wrong, turned their faith into one focussed on truth at the expense of all else. They'd forgotten about loving Jesus and loving those who didn't know God. Jesus says to the believers, *"you have abandoned the love you had at first"* (v4). Unfortunately history has had a habit of repeating itself. Through the ages people have been treated poorly by those with influence saying they follow God, when in fact they have abandoned Him.

So, much like the search for that lost item, Jesus says, *"Remember therefore from where you have fallen"* (v5). Every one of us needs to ask ourselves the question, "Is my love for Jesus and others the same as it was at the start?" If you've realised that the answer is "no," it's possible to rediscover this love. Start by retracing your steps. Think back to the times when you were so interested in Jesus, that you could call it love. Your heart was on fire, there was life in your bones and you were full of love for those who didn't know Jesus too. Stop and think for a moment. Do you remember a time like that? What good things were you doing that fuelled this love? What things caused you to lose that love? Did something come in as a distraction, preventing you from seeing Jesus as number one? The Ephesian Church were so into being right, calling out the wrong in others that they couldn't love the person who was in need of grace. Every one of us is in need of the undeserved favour of God.

What about you? How do you feel when someone posts something online that you don't think is right? Are you ready to take them down? Before you type a word, ask Jesus, "How do you see that person?" Jesus wants you and me to re-discover a love for Him. When our love for Jesus grows we begin to see others the way He sees them; and that is with a love that doesn't quit. True faith comes from a living relationship with the Lord Jesus as He is revealed through the Bible. Over the page is a prayer space if you would like to spend time thinking deeper on this with Jesus...

31

From what we've read, it's clear that Jesus wants to put back into our hearts a joy and a love for Him. It's something He wants even more than we do! So be confident that He will meet you in this moment...

1) As you play a worship song, add to this word-mix any words that remind you of Jesus (no matter how random!):

2) Think about God's love for you and write a note of thanks to Jesus.

3) Is there anyone that you need to forgive? This is releasing any hard feelings and hate that you have for this person. Tell Jesus about it and hand your bitterness over for Jesus to deal with. The space here is to write something that will remind you of your choice to forgive this person or people today.

4) Has anything come in to distract you from Jesus? Does something else have first place in your heart? What about the time spent on your device or social media? Maybe a relationship has come between you and your relationship with Jesus? Maybe you want to make a promise to Jesus about something:

5) Seeing others the way Jesus sees them. Ask the Lord to show you someone who doesn't yet know Him. Ask Jesus to show you what He loves about that person. Maybe you would like to commit to pray for this person? Why not write their name here:

TRUE VALUE

Revelation 2:8-11

Imagine you wake up one day deciding that you're going to take a year out of your busy life, to help needy people living in remote the places of South America. However, after thinking about it for a while, you remember that you are scared of snakes. So to calm any fears you might have about snakes, you do a little research. You come across some interesting reading, from an old Peace Corps Manual.[a] It details what to do to survive, if confronted by a hungry anaconda in the Amazonian jungle:

- Do not run. The snake is faster than you are.
- Lie flat on the ground, put your arms tight against your sides and your legs tight against each other.
- Tuck your chin in.
- The snake will begin to nudge and climb over your body
- Do not panic
- The snake will begin to swallow you, feet first.
- You must lie perfectly still. This will take a long time.
- When the snake reaches your knees, reach down, take your knife, slide it into the side of the snake's mouth, between the edge of its mouth and your leg.
- Quickly rip upward, severing the snake's head.
- Be sure you have a knife.
- Be sure it is sharp.

So the question today is: what would you be willing to lay your life down for? In the part we read today, we discovered the church in Smyrna was facing a time of life-threatening dangers. This location was a centre for the Empire where it was a requirement to worship the Roman Emperor Domitian. Yet as a Christian, you cannot truly say "Jesus is Lord," if with your next breath you say "Caesar is Lord." Jewish leaders in Smyrna seized upon this opportunity to inform on the Christians, adding false accusations to their reports. Those arrested were imprisoned. Here they would await trial before being sentenced to forced labour, deportation, or death.

Understanding their troubles Jesus says, *"I know your tribulation"* (v9). It's a real comfort when God reveals to us what He knows about our lives. It shows that we haven't been forgotten. You have not been forgotten! Be reassured that your situation isn't some random mess. God is in charge.

Yet something is required of all Christians who face the challenges ahead, *"Be faithful unto death, and I will give you the crown of life"* (v10). This is where the real test comes. Often we're going to be faced with tough choices; decisions that test how important Jesus is to us. If faced with having to give up something for Jesus, how would you react? Would you choose to preserve the hopes and plans you have for your future? Would you give up a relationship, a lifestyle, or even your life? This isn't a one off message from Jesus. It's confirmed in Matt 16:26, *"What will it profit a man if he gains the whole world and forfeits his soul?"* Much like the anaconda story; the laying down of your life is actually the way of saving it. Survival comes by submitting to God's way, even when it's one we don't quite understand.

"But how can You ask this of me Jesus?" We ask. Remember, He knows our situation inside out. He is *"The first and the last, who died,"* (v8). He was falsely accused, arrested and put to death. He went through similar trials for us. Just as Jesus' trials were followed by being raised from the dead, so "the crown of life" is promised to those who are faithful to Him. This is the prize for holding true to Jesus. The people of Smyrna would be familiar with this idea. Much like the prize of a laurel wreath given to Olympian winners; athletes competed not for gold, but for a status that money could not buy. An eternal reward with the promise of avoiding *"the second death"* will be ours when we've proved ourselves faithful.

Maybe you want to know more about how to receive this promise of eternal life? Over the page is a prayer space to help guide you through.

The Bible tells us that God so loved the world (that is us), that He gave His only Son that whoever believes in Him shall not perish but have everlasting life (John 3:16).

Q - Do you believe that God came to earth for you?
Q - Do you believe that Jesus lived and died for you?
Q - Do you believe that God loves you?

The Bible says that no one is perfect; that we have all done wrong and fallen short of God's standard. Heaven is a perfect place where God is, but we being imperfect are separated from God without Jesus.

Q - Do you admit that you have done wrong?
Q - Are you sorry for those things you have done?
Q - Would you like God to forgive you?

The Bible contains eye witness accounts of how the Romans executed Jesus through the torture of nailing Him to a cross (John 19). God purposed this to happen so that ours wrongs could be erased. He rose from the dead three days later demonstrating that He was God's Son (John 20).

Q – Do you believe Jesus was God's only Son?
Q – Do you believe that He died for you?
Q – Do you believe He rose from the dead?

Jesus said "Whoever wants to become my disciple must deny themselves and take up their cross and follow me." (Matthew 16:24).

Q – Will you receive God's free gift of wrongs forgiven and eternal life with Him in heaven?
Q – Do you choose to live your life for Jesus?

Whether you've been to church loads of times or never set foot inside a church, God wants you to know Him. When you pray this prayer something will happen. God will come close to you whether you sense Him close or not. He wants you to know that you are His forever!

If you have chosen to follow Jesus, please pray this prayer...

> *Dear Lord God; Almighty God, I come to You as a stranger, but I want to be Your friend.*
>
> *I know that in Your deep love for me You welcome me. Thank You for sending Jesus into the world to show me what You are like. I believe He is Your Son and that He lived on this earth and that He was executed by the Romans. Thank You that You planned this in order that I could be made free; free from the power of the enemy over my life and free to be forgiven for all of my wrongs.*
>
> *I believe Jesus rose from the dead and that I can know Him with me every day.*
>
> *Please forgive me for all the wrong things that I have done. I am truly sorry. In respect for You, I turn away from the wrong things I have done and choose to follow You. Help me to live my life for You.*
>
> *Now I ask You to come and take over my heart and my life. In Jesus' name!*

Once you have taken this step with God, the Bible calls you a child of God *"Yet to all who did receive Him, to those who believed in His name, He gave the right to become children of God"* (John 1:12). This means that you have peace with God; and God as the best loving Father includes you in His family and will guide you in life, protect you and provide for the things you need. This is the start of a wonderful friendship with God!

#Day8

STUMBLING BLOCKS

Revelation 2:12-17

I think we can learn a lot from action movies. You know, things you wouldn't be able to practice in everyday life, but would be really handy to know in an emergency... Did you know that you don't actually need a pick to access a locked door? Just give it a good kick and it'll cave in easily. Ever outnumbered in a martial arts fight? The odds are still okay though. Your assailants will wait their turn to attack you, charging in mindlessly to connect their face with your fist! You'll also be able to knock them out with one punch too, so no need to worry about them getting up a second time to attack you! Obviously you're fully aware that the use of air vents is the only way to escape undetected from any industrial facility!

It's not over once you're outside though; don't forget there's always a chase! This is actually handy to know. If you're being chased on foot, be it by dogs, ninjas or zombies, there's an easy way to slow their progress. As you pass large objects such as bins, rickshaws or market stalls, give them a pull, so that they crash into the path of your pursuers. Maybe your assailants will give up the chase after falling over one too many giant pots! Although, they'll likely be replaced by an angry mob of townspeople, chasing you for the things you destroyed in the process of your escape!

In a race, stumbling over can take a while to recover from. I don't know if you're familiar with the concept of stumbling in your faith. It's referred to in verse 14 with a reference to an Old Testament man, Balaam, *"who taught Balak (king of Moab) to put a stumbling block before the sons of Israel."* The king of Moab saw the Israelites as his enemy and wanted to bring them down; but he knew he couldn't beat them in a head-on battle. So he offered Balaam money to curse them. Balaam refused, but later on advised Balak on a sly way to harm God's people. The Israelites would spot an attack of an army, but they would not so easily detect the threat of being led astray by the Moabite women. Their affection for the Moabite women, led them to compromise their dedication to God, choosing to be involved in the rituals of other gods.

In the bit we read, the followers of Jesus in Pergamum are living in what could be described as a spiritual battle-zone. Under the Imperial rule of the Romans, a large Acropolis housed temples of worship to Greek gods. One such god called Asclepius was hailed as the healing and saving god. People would participate in rituals invoking demonic powers in order to receive dreams or visions whilst snakes slithered through the rooms. During the reign of Nero, the church in Pergamum resisted all attempts to deny their faith in Jesus. Antipas, the Bishop of Pergamum was martyred by pagan priests there for his ministry of casting out evil spirits.

There was though, another strategy at work: a stumbling block or trap that was altogether more subtle. Much like the Israelites' affections for other women had led them astray, so an attitude of compromise had spread to God's people. "Idol sacrifices aren't a big deal, are they?" some thought. "Don't you know they take place all the time?" Many a feast involved such practices, but led to much more besides. They had held fast against persecution, but did not do so well when it came to temptation.

Faithfulness to God involves both loyalty and obedience. Jesus's sacrifice bought for us a purity of heart at a very high price. This is something to be valued and guarded, rather than treated as optional. Compromising our purity will hinder the growth of our faith and relationship with God as well as our witness to others. It's easy to be misled into thinking if everyone is doing something, that it's okay for us too. Can you recognise the subtle ways that the enemy is trying to bring you down in your faith?

Jesus' method of rescue for us is forgiveness of our wrongs! He calls us, to change our ways, *"Therefore repent"* (v16). This is not to condemn or humiliate us, but the way we can be saved from falling over and never getting up again. The words, *"and I will give him a white stone,"* (17) describe the innocence that Jesus offers in return, when we change from moral compromise and turn back to Him. So hold fast!

TO THE ONE WHO CONQUERS I WILL GIVE SOME

of the hidden manna,

AND I WILL GIVE A WHITE STONE,

with a new name written on

THE STONE THAT NO ONE KNOWS EXCEPT

the one who receives it.

#Day9

UNDER THE INFLUENCE

Revelation 2:18-29

Have you heard that the average person swallows eight spiders per year? No? Are you freaked out? Don't worry, because it's not actually true. It's one of those stories known as an "Urban myth." Someone has been told a piece of information as a science fact, when it's actually a load of made-up nonsense that sounds like it could be true. In fact, our face is quite sensitive. Even when asleep, it will react to the feeling of something crawling over it. Ever been told that a spider is more scared of you, than you are of it? Spiders do not have a death wish to crawl into your mouth, any more than Lando Calrissian wanted to see inside the giant mouth of the Sarlaac in the Star Wars film "Return of the Jedi."

Maybe you've never believed the spider story (or just been told it was less spiders!). Well then... Did you know that tapping a can of fizzy drink won't prevent the contents from spilling over; and eating carrots won't actually make you see in the dark? "Hang on a second!" You might say. "I've been deceived! I've been tapping my fizzy drinks cans for years!" It's obviously not a big deal, but if you've done that or been eating carrots to see at night (when it doesn't work), you'll feel wrongly influenced.

In the bit we read, a woman who is nicknamed "Jezebel" has gained influence and is misleading a group of God's people with false ideas. Claiming special knowledge, she takes up the status of a prophet to convince people into believing that some ungodly practices are okay. Her words are manipulative; and like a seductive poison that controls, people are falling for it. Jesus opens with, *"The words of the Son of God, who has eyes like a flame of fire"* (v18). This is the only time in the book of Revelation that Jesus is referred to as the Son of God, showing that His authority is greater than the one trying to exert power over others. His response to this "Jezebel" is "Did you think I wouldn't notice??? Turn away from your false teachings that are misleading others!" With eyes like a flame of fire, not only can Jesus see how she was misleading people, but also her refusal to stop deceiving people. By calling her "Jezebel," Jesus is showing how she is operating like the Old Testament Queen who was known for her evil deeds and ways of manipulation and control of others.

This is happening among a group of God's people that were doing really well. They've demonstrated love, faith, service and perseverance (v19), which any group of believers would be thankful for. Even better, some are continuing to grow in these ways. Unfortunately they've also allowed a false prophet to gain status within their church, and she is beginning to control others. It could be that she was using paranormal means to charm people in to thinking she had some special connection to God. But the important question has to be: How can I tell whether I'm being led by God or misled by evil? Ask yourself this question: Does its outcome lead to the loving and obeying of Jesus, to selflessly putting others first and of the patient endurance mentioned in verse 19? The teaching by some there led to the very opposite! Clearly these words did not come from God.

Like urban myths, it's possible to be taken in by popular ideas that sound reasonable, but are actually poison. Therefore the Lord is stepping in, to bring judgement to "Jezebel" and her children (meaning her followers). Sometimes it's necessary to confront those, who falsely lay claim to leadership positions clearly not given by God. Verse 27 shows the perfect balance of a leader. *"And He will rule them with a rod of iron,"* is taken from Psalm 2:9, but is not the harsh idea of governing strictly. The word for "rule" here actually means "tend" as a shepherd leads his sheep. The rod is an unbreakable staff, which carefully guides the sheep, but strikes those intending to do harm. People of Thyatira would have recognised the picture language of pottery, since clay was used as moulds to cast bronze statues of false gods. One day, these casts would be shattered; and with them the controlling power and influence over the people.

Lord Jesus. You are the bright and morning star, the Lord who brings victory out of the darkest of times. You are the light of the world. Amen!

i know your works,
YOUR LOVE AND FAITH
and service and patient
ENDURANCE

#Day10

AWAKE!

Revelation 3:1-6

Imagine that something really incredible happens in your day. It starts off as one of those ordinary days, when suddenly the unbelievable takes place. Say, a video that you produce and post on YouTube gets two hundred million views, or your school bus driver faints at the wheel whilst driving, and you manage to get to the driving seat and stop the bus, rescuing the forty passengers. You'd be thrilled by such an amazing event; but how would you make sure that it wasn't all a dream? What would you do to check you aren't just asleep? Would you pinch yourself? Does that actually wake someone up, if your dream-self pinches your own arm? Do you ask yourself, "Is this a dream?" Does the awareness of a dream stop the dream from occurring? The best way to be woken up from a dream is if someone who is awake calls to you in a loud voice. The words, "Breakfast is ready!!" or "You're late for school!!" will probably do it.

The followers of Jesus in Sardis are in need of this kind of shock treatment, *"Wake up!!"* (v2). A gentle whisper won't do it. These words might come across as harsh, but it's possible to miss what it is to be a Christian. Following Jesus is about having a faith in Him that is alive. Why do you talk to God? Is it because you feel you have to; or do you really want to connect with Him? Praying is so much more than "hands together, eyes closed, say after me." It's a conversation with God, using everyday words and sometimes no words at all! Did you know that you can just ask God to be with you and lay down in the quiet? It's also important to read His words in the Bible. He will use those to speak to you. Perhaps you want to write God a letter or draw, sing or dance as you become inspired by Him.

The people at Sardis had *"the works"* (v1). They were busy doing the "God stuff," but somewhere along the way, they'd lost their connection to Him. Jesus comes to them with the *"sevenfold Spirit and the seven angels"* (v1).

He has everything they lack. The Holy Spirit makes the church complete and connects us with the activity of heaven. Jesus wants to revive this group of believers, not condemn them; yet if the shock of His words doesn't wake them up, He will no longer be for them, but against them.

So Jesus says *"Remember, then, what you received and heard."* When they began they would have received the Holy Spirit and seen Him at work, speaking through them, changing lives and showing up in powerful ways. "Remember that?" Jesus says. They were complete when they began. Yet somehow now they didn't seem to think that the powerful workings of God in people's lives mattered, compared to the business of church tasks and rules. I used to think the Holy Spirit was just a religious word people used in a blessing, until I experienced Him fill my heart like a fire.

Jesus comes and offers you and me the Holy Spirit to help us (see John 14:15-27). The Holy Spirit will make the words you read in the Bible come to life. He will also show you what Jesus is like, helping you to understand how real He is and help you do the things He did. Being a follower of Jesus is a relationship that is deeper than a friendship. As our Lord, He wants to lovingly guide and encourage us every day with something new. We have to want this to take place, inviting Him to come close each day.

Unfortunately, it's possible to let distractions take away the time that we might otherwise devote to God. The Holy Spirit has an important role in our lives as He keeps us updated with Jesus and the Father. Being alert to what can lead us away from God is important. Sardis was known for its citadel built on a mountain. It was said to be impossible for an army to successfully attack it. Yet because the place had this reputation, those living there had a careless attitude to security, resulting in it being overcome twice. Jesus sounded the alarm to people of the day; yet His words are also for us. Pinch yourself! Are you awake? How do you know if you are awake? When did you last take time to be close to God, to discover more of Him? When did His words connect with your heart?

Over the page is an opportunity for you to take time out with God and to allow the Holy Spirit to bring about a spiritual awakening to your heart.

Have you ever said to Jesus, "Lord. I'm here. I want to meet with You. I'll wait for You. I'll be with you as long as You want"?

Why not come to Jesus with that attitude now?

Inviting the Holy Spirit

Jesus wants you to receive the Holy Spirit (John 14:15-17).
Ask the Holy Spirit to show you more of Jesus and Father God.

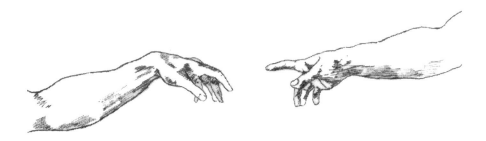

Waiting for the Holy Spirit

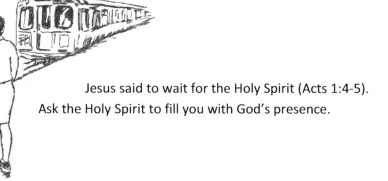

Jesus said to wait for the Holy Spirit (Acts 1:4-5).
Ask the Holy Spirit to fill you with God's presence.

What is God saying to you?

Ask the Lord to show you something more about what He's like.

Ask the Lord to show you something He loves about you.

What is your response to Him?

#Day11
KEEP GOING
Revelation 3:7-13

Ever had the desire to get up early and do a run on a Saturday morning? I know the thought of leaving a comfy bed when it's not a school day is just wrong, but these days it can be a fun community experience. Whatever your ability, you turn up at 9:30am, to walk, jog or run for five kilometres. At the finish, you're given a token which registers the time of your completed run. As the weeks go by, you get used to pushing yourself in a bid to beat your own personal best time.

There is, however one part of the run that no one is fond of. It's called "the hill," situated just after the half-way point. The hill is a long gradual climb, which gets steeper and steeper, transforming you into a slow motion version of yourself. Halfway into the ascent, your lungs ask you where all the oxygen has gone, your legs appear to double in weight, and you wonder if in fact you are still moving forward. Gasping for air, you question how on earth anyone could put the words "fun" and "run" into the same sentence? The temptation to stop and rest becomes the only thing you can think of, along with the question "Who's idea was it to do this on a Saturday?" Noticing that you are struggling, one of your fellow runners will ask if you're okay. Having experienced the same difficulties, they'll often speak encouraging words to help you carry on. "Come on! Keep going! You can do it! It's not far to go!" Who can ever ignore words like that? So on you go, determined to make it to the end!

Sometimes, this mission that we're given to "go and make disciples" can feel like an uphill struggle. We can appear to have little influence and at times are labelled unfairly. The followers of Jesus in Philadelphia, had been discredited and outnumbered by a strong group from the local Jewish synagogue. It was most likely that God's people were expelled from the Jewish community and identified as a dangerous sect, making them vulnerable to unjust imprisonment and worse from the Romans. Yet this small band of followers with *"little power"* (v8) were remaining faithful, keeping to the teachings of Jesus, even though their very identity was being brought into question.

Jesus begins by setting the record straight, stating that He, the Lord, is the *"true one, who has the key of David"* (v7). Jewish heritage was secured on the Kingdom of David. King Jesus, born of David's line, encourages the Christians that they do indeed have a right to be a part of God's kingdom. Jesus reinforces this by stating that they also had access to God's heavenly resources as an open door, connecting them to heaven now through prayer and beyond into eternal life. As His faithful followers we too have an open door of special access, with opportunities for us to bring heaven into the lives others. It's important to keep to His word. Others might replace God's truth with lies; but the power of heaven is only released when we stick to His words as we step into the unknown.

When times are tough, we need to remember our identity. Jesus reminds us that we belong to Him. He is the true Messiah, about whom it was prophesied throughout the history of God's people. We are His. We are connected to heaven. In the uphill struggles that you face, when it feels like you can't go on, Jesus is running next to you. He wants you to succeed. He's saying "Keep going. We're in this together! It's not far to go! Your reward ahead is a crown of life!"

Jesus uses the words *"the hour"* (v10), to refer to events that indicate the very end of something. At the end of time there will be times of testing, but Jesus reassures us that He is returning. Like a pillar that stands the test of time, still standing, even after the shock of an earthquake, so those who persevere, will honour God in His temple. His encouragement to you today, in uncertain times is "Keep going. You will make it through."

King Jesus. I thank You that I am a part of Your Kingdom and I know that in the middle of struggle, I have all that I need. My identity is in You. My confidence is in You. I trust You with all that is to come.

HOLD FAST
what you have,
SO THAT NO ONE MAY
sieze your crown.

#Day12

ANSWER THE DOOR

Revelation 3:14-22

Do you have a best friend that you've had for years? Maybe they live down your street or sit next to you at school? Now imagine it's the sort of friendship where you're always seen with each other and that you both enjoy listening to music together. Your friend is particularly good at singing, so you often play songs on YouTube, singing along karaoke style.

One day, after an unforgettable night watching the Eurovision song contest, you make a special vow where you promise to always be together to watch Eurovision. Years later, after singing a karaoke song in public with you, your best friend is approached by an agent. To cut a long story short, they land themselves a record deal. You are genuinely pleased for your pal. Secretly you are their biggest fan! After a while though, you notice them beginning to drift from your life. You often text, but the replies become less frequent. Their new lifestyle has afforded them a new house, to which you have yet to be invited.

Then, you see it on the television... the Eurovision song contest is on next weekend!! Remembering your unbreakable promise, you excitedly call your mate in order to make arrangements for the night. Unfortunately when they answer the phone, your friend doesn't seem to be that bothered. They respond by saying that their friends aren't really into Eurovision, so they won't be able to make it. "But this is the Eurovision song contest," you tell your buddy. To which they reply, "Meh." You hear laughing in the background; they've had you on speakerphone with their new friends. "You know what???" you reply, "You make me sick!!"

It takes a lot to say something like this to someone you love, but in a similar way Jesus says this to some in the church (v16). We have a picture of Jesus knocking on the door, *"Behold I stand at the door and knock"* (v20), inviting His people to come and make a commitment with Him. Whilst shutting Jesus out of their lives, some had taken the view that being a disciple was about a lifestyle of comfort. Being handily located on a crossing, linking three main trade routes, they had access to all they needed in terms of money and fine clothes. Yet there was an underlying attitude problem that was making them ineffective as followers of Jesus.

It's easy to mistake Jesus' words about being *"neither cold nor hot"* (v15), to mean that Jesus would rather they were "cold-hearted" than lukewarm. Archaeology has discovered that the people of Laodicea accessed their water from two sources. One came via an aqueduct 12 miles east, where cool fresh water originated. The other water supply reached them from hot springs 6 miles away. Yet due to the distance, both water sources arrived lukewarm to the people. Neither was useful; either as cool refreshing water, or a hot soothing bath. The Laodicean believers were now so distant from Jesus that they were not of any benefit to those around them. Their lifestyle of wealth had made them less concerned for matters of the soul. They knew neither the refreshing peace of God to save souls, or the soothing love of God which brought healing.

We have to take the challenges of Jesus personally and ask ourselves those uncomfortable questions. What do I value the most? Is Jesus challenging me to give anything up as I follow Him? Am I allowing an easy Christianity to take over my life, where I don't think that God demands anything from me? To ignore such questions is to ignore the voice of God. This can lead to a distance growing between us and God. If we're not taking the challenge of Jesus seriously, we'll likely not make a difference to the lives of others. At the same time we'll also put our own soul at risk.

When mined, gold has to go through the intense heat of refining in order to become useful and beautiful. When we submit to the challenges of Jesus, and stick with Him through the tough times, we become like gold refined by fire. Through this process Jesus makes our character beautiful. We gain the wisdom to see which things of this earth are really of true value. Will you answer the door to allow Jesus to work in your life again?

BEHOLD, I STAND AT
the door and knock.
IF ANYONE
hears my voice
AND OPENS
the door,
I WILL COME IN
and eat with him.
AND HE WITH ME.

GOD IS IN CHARGE

Revelation 4:1-11

When a friend invites you to their house, it can be a special opportunity to get to know them a bit more than you might at school. You're with them in their space, which can tell you a lot about what a person is like. For a start, their bedroom will have a different vibe to yours. You'll instantly notice posters on the walls, books they've read, things they are into and whether or not they are musical. Are they a tidy person with special items on display; maybe fairy lights and a study area? Or are they less organised, with an overflowing bin and a pile of their favourite tops randomly scattered? Seeing their own style, furniture, and layout, gives you a glimpse into how they operate from day to day.

Along with John we get a glimpse of God's room. The word "Revelation" comes from the Greek word "apocalypse," which instantly brings to mind burnt skies, clouds of smoke, and devastation. Yet the word apocalypse actually means an "unveiling" where we receive insight into the unseen realm of heaven and of *"the things which must take place"* (v1).

John writes, *"I looked and behold, a door standing open in heaven!"* (v1). Here we get a sighting of the throne room of God. And much like being in your friend's room, John discovers more of what God is like. As he speaks about what Jesus shows him, can you tell that he's attempting to describe the indescribable? So John uses phrases such as *"had the appearance of"* (v3) and *"as it were"* (v6) or *"like a…"* (v7) to give you an idea of what he felt as well as what he saw. Immediately his eyes are drawn to the centre of it all, the throne. The LORD is sitting there, who shines like the beauty of precious jewels, displaying both His majesty as King and His supernatural character. Surrounding God is a full circle rainbow, revealing that God holds to the promises He has made with His people (Genesis 9:13).

What else originates from the throne? As *"flashes of lightning, rumblings and peals of thunder"* come, John would have felt the awesome power of God. Vibrating through John's chest, with more intensity than a bass speaker at a music gig; the rumblings of God's voice show how He is active and full of authority and power.

The elders that surround the throne are priestly figures, representatives between God and His people. As leaders of the twelve tribes of Israel and of the church (the twelve apostles), the white clothes given them by God show they've been made clean. The gold crowns honour their royal status, as a reward from God for their faithful service through the hardships they've faced. As an act of worship, the elders fall before the LORD, signifying an attitude of complete submission. They throw their crowns before God, recognising that their good deeds were not theirs alone, but accomplished by the help of God.

It makes sense for the God of the living to be worshiped by four angelic living creatures, with eyes that see the works of God taking place all over the earth. Seen flying above a sea of crystal which represents the place where heaven and earth meet, in Ezekiel 1:22 they are seen flying below it whilst on the earth. They likely represent creation; coming from the north, south, east and west, declaring that God is holy and worthy. This word "holy" tells us that God is both immortal and pure and that He detests evil. The song about God's worthiness is that He is the Creator God who keeps everything in existence from day to day (v11). We can join in with this song, since we exist because God wanted it.

God is the centre of it all. We are shown that He is the King upon the throne, One who is all-powerful and uses that power rightly. This sight is to prepare us for the events that must take place. As the battles on earth and heaven intensify, God's plans will come to pass. We may go through some trials and struggles, but the view in heaven shows us that God is still in charge. God is on the throne. Evil will be overcome.

Holy, holy, holy; Father, Son and Holy Spirit, I adore You. Creator God. Thank You for making me worthy to come into your space. In Jesus' name.

#prayerspace

On the page opposite are different starting points for talking to God.

Maybe after what you have just read, you want to offer something heartfelt to God? Why not look up and play the song "So will I (100 Billion X)" ©Hillsong Music Publishing. Perhaps you feel inspired to write a poem, or simply to sing a song you know. There's space on both pages to write or draw around the pictures as you feel inspired to. Sometimes I just listen to a song and start drawing shapes as I consider God and Him being close to me. Often the results are surprising! Why not give it a try?!

May my meditation on Your words

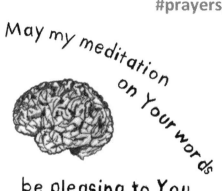

be pleasing to You

What is it that You are saying to me?

It's Your breath in my lungs

So I'll pour out my praise to You

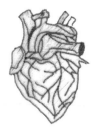

I'll bring You more than a song

What can I give

Lord I give You my heart

to You my King?

#Day14

SET FREE

Revelation 5:1-14

Some years ago, we had a drawer in our house that had a very special purpose. So significant was this drawer, it was even given the name: "The Important Drawer." All would know it was not just any drawer! What was inside this drawer of significance? It certainly wasn't cluttered up with lowly objects such as the odd key (unless it was an important key), a pair of sunglasses, or a phone charger. No, this drawer was reserved for essential items, which if lost would cause us a lot of bother.

What items were special enough to make it into the "Important Drawer"? Documents of course! You know the kind, plane tickets, applications and original birth certificates. I have a feeling a lottery ticket may even have made it into the important drawer once! No it wasn't a winner!

Important documents form a key part of our lives. They can work for us, giving us access to further opportunities. Having your final exam results officially recorded on paper provide proof to potential employers of your achievements. Legal documents are required for getting married, buying a car or moving house. In the part we read today, the LORD is holding an important document, a scroll, which is held back by a legal condition that prevents it from being opened. The moment John discovers this, he weeps uncontrollably, because he sees that this scroll relates to the completion of God's rescue plan for humanity. The situation appears hopeless. A legally binding agreement, established not by a signature, but by the eating of an apple, saw evil take its hold on humanity (Genesis 3).

The scroll contains an unveiling of actions which *"must take place"* (Rev. 4:1). Its opening will enable the contents to be read aloud and trigger the events recorded in the scroll to take place. Who then is honourable and deserving enough to break the power of the legal agreement made between mankind and the enemy, which hangs over this scroll?

John is told that the *"Lion of the tribe of Judah has conquered"* (v5). This title is given to the Messiah, the one of whom it was predicted would save humankind. This is Jesus. John expects to see a majestic, strong and powerful creature; but instead reports a helpless little lamb standing before the throne, with the appearance of having been killed. At the time of Jesus, many of God's people expected to see the Messiah overthrow the Romans with a strong show of God's power. Yet God's plan was one of a very different nature. First an unseen power had to be overthrown. Humankind was under the power of an enemy, through an agreement that came about when Adam and Eve chose Satan's way instead of God's.

The descendants of Adam and Eve are like those captured in war in need of rescue, *"for by your blood you ransomed people for God"* (v9). It is recorded that in ancient times, those captured and taken by the Romans after battle were able to be released for a fee. Often individuals would be set free once the ransom money had been paid. Although strong and powerful as the "Lion of Judah," Jesus submitted Himself as payment for mankind through His slaughter by Roman execution. We can be free from the power of the devil, who uses sin (wrong doing) to enslave us.

I'm sure you've noticed something unusual about this lamb. How many slaughtered lambs do you see standing out in the fields, moving about? This Lamb has been resurrected to life again! Jesus is living! King Jesus, the Lion of Judah, has gone through the extreme suffering of death by Roman execution, paying the price to buy us out of slavery. Who could be more worthy than Him to now unleash God's vengeance against Satan and all evil?! So like a magistrate in a courtroom the LORD hands the Lamb the scroll to be opened, so that *"what must take place"* can begin.

Maybe you can see why sin is so damaging to our lives? Giving into evil is submitting to the control of the enemy. It can lead to bad habits and bad choices that are hard to break free from. God's judgment on sin is death, but His love for us brings release and freedom that leads to eternal life.

In Revelation 5:8 the living creatures and elders are each holding a harp. This represents a worship of God that is all about who God is, what He is like and what He has done for us. Worship leads us deeper into the heart of God. When worship is paired with prayer it makes a powerful combination.

As you take time with God write, doodle or draw what comes to mind...

YOUR WAYS IN THE BIBLE

THINGS YOU HAVE DONE FOR ME

HOW YOU ARE DESCRIBED IN THE BIBLE

TO ME YOU ARE LIKE

The holding up of a bowl of incense here represents the prayers of the saints, rising like smoke up to heaven. When mixed with true worship, faith rises within and our prayers are powerfully answered.

LET YOUR KiNGDOM COME

#Day15

THE FOUR HORSEMEN

Revelation 6:1-4

I remember the day of our rush to hospital. With a twenty five minute drive ahead of us, the thought foremost in my mind was, "Would we make it in time?" As I raced down the road, every traffic light that approached was a challenge to be beaten. In my desperation, I half hoped that we would pass a Police car, as a Police escort would save us precious minutes.

We had phoned ahead to the hospital, so they would be ready for our arrival. As I burst through the entrance announcing that we had arrived, staff seemed to have a little less urgency than I was comfortable with. I guess they had seen it all before, parents-to-be expecting their first child. Oh did I forget to mention that? My wife Debs and I were having our first baby. Of course we were ready for this, with coins for the car park meter, an overnight bag with nappies, wipes, chocolate and magazines.

So when we arrived at the hospital and informed them that the baby was coming, we were told to wait, before being settled into a room. I don't know what I was expecting it to be like, but the baby did not pop out in the next five minutes. He did not arrive in the next hour, or three hours, or even eight hours! It also turned out that magazines were not really of much interest when you are experiencing the pains of labour every five to ten minutes. It's not like waiting for a bus I can tell you! It is very painful at very regular intervals! The chocolate was very tasty though.

What we read in this part of Revelation is often referred to as "The four horsemen of the apocalypse," which can be a bit misleading. It's as if people are expecting to see actual riders coming from the clouds on the day of judgement, releasing a sequence of future catastrophes. Yet we read yesterday that a scroll containing these events was opened by Jesus the Lamb following His death and resurrection. The seals have already been opened. These things are already taking place. Our world is being impacted by what Jesus refers to as "birth pains" (Matthew 24:4-14). As in the pains of childbirth, a delay takes place before the final event. Yet these signs are here to leave us in no doubt that we are in the last days.

Notice that the four horsemen are "given permission" to bring suffering to this world. Evil wants to have its way in this world but is held back by God. The first rider actually bears a similarity to a vision of Jesus that John sees later on in Revelation; but here it is not Jesus. This rider carries a bow, which stands for the evil leadership of those who abuse their positions of power to take over those who are weaker than they are. The crown represents ruling powers, not satisfied with leading their own people, they successfully conquer other unwilling nations by force too.

The second rider brings war, where nations join forces to fight against other nations. This horse is as red as blood. The great sword stands for the large amount of lives lost on the field of battle. Countries that once enjoyed peace are thrown into turmoil. People flee as bombs are dropped on their homes and innocent lives are lost.

Seeing these things happen in the world can lead us to ask, "Where is God? Why is there so much suffering in this world?" In the last two devotions we have clearly seen that God is on the throne. He is in charge. But how does this make sense, when the horrors that come through war are so destructive? Why doesn't God do something about it? Our world is in the pains of labour. These things are a sign post, revealing the fact that something is coming. The evil which humankind invited into this world has caused its devastation. It is God who holds this world together. To a world that resists the LORD and His Lamb, this is a small taste of what it would look like without Him if evil were allowed to have its way. This view from heaven gives us a very different perspective on our lives!

Everlasting God. You are still in charge. I look to You. You are the Creator who brought this world into being. Your purposes are being worked out in my lifetime. Help me to see things like You do. In Jesus Name.

i watched when

THE LAMB OPENED ONE OF THE SEVEN SEALS

#journalspace

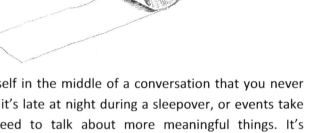

#Day16

A GLOBAL CRISIS

Revelation 6:5-8

Do you ever find yourself in the middle of a conversation that you never thought likely? Maybe it's late at night during a sleepover, or events take place that see the need to talk about more meaningful things. It's surprising how open people are to chat about spiritual things when the opportunity presents itself.

A friend of mine, Jeff was at work one day, when a conversation with a work colleague got round to the subject of God. After talking about how Jesus had made all the difference in his life, Jeff asked, "What about you? Do you want to give your life to Jesus?" His work mate replied "I have a beautiful wife, a lovely house and a new Toyota, why do I need God?" To which Jeff replied, "What about your deepest, darkest thoughts. Who's going to forgive you for those my friend, your Toyota?"

When life becomes comfortable, people assume there's less of a need for God. Like the church in Laodicea we read about in *#Day12*, humankind has become self-sufficient. When we have all we need in terms of health, relationships, finance, and leisure; we can become distracted from the need for God in our lives. Yet in times of hardship or risk to well-being, those necessary questions about God suddenly become more important.

In the part we read today, John witnesses the release of two further horsemen. Although the seals are referred to as first, second, third and fourth, the trials that come from the horsemen are not meant to be understood as events that happen one after the other on earth. They are signs of the last days, but it's not like you can tick them off one by one on a sheet to work out how close the end is. Although the fact that our world has been experiencing these events in increasing measure, is significant.

The rider on a black horse carries a pair of scales. These are not scales of justice, but weighing scales, used in a market to measure out portions of food for sale. This represents a time of famine and poverty, as crops fail due to extreme weather conditions. *"A quart of wheat"* was a day's ration of food for one person and *"a denarius"* was a day's wages. This reflects food shortages and a sharp rise in the price of food. Imagine your Big Mac and fries costing eight hour's work! The cheaper option was to buy *"three quarts of barley for a denarius"* and mix it with a little wheat to make the food go further. In AD 92 a shortage from the grain harvest caused a food crisis, prompting the Roman Emperor to order that corn be grown at the expense of wine production. These are events outside of human control.

The pale horse of a yellowish-green colour describes a sickness that covers the earth, with an increase in naturally occurring disasters which cause a high death toll. The television news regularly reports of calamities caused by tornados, tsunamis or wildfires. A significant crisis that dominated the world's attention for much of 2020 was the Covid-19 global pandemic, where the world was told to stay indoors. Hundreds of thousands of people died through contracting this contagious virus. Surprisingly, as people hit the shops to stock up on essential items for this time of lockdown, it seemed that one 24 pack of toilet rolls just wasn't enough!

As initial reports began to spread of new cases being detected across the globe there was an increase in searches on Google for "prayer." Online prayer requests grew as people realised that with no vaccines and no cures, there was a limit even to what our experienced and dedicated medical staff could achieve.

It's moments like these when we realise we need God. These are desperate times where the Lord is trying to get our attention before it's too late. As when birth pains lead to the birth of a child, so these events will lead to the return of Christ. Some have asked, "Did God cause the virus?" Others have asked "Why did God not prevent it?" I expect there have been many calamities that the Lord has prevented that we will never know about. Yet God loves us too much to allow us to stay comfy but uninformed about the eternal peril which He is trying to save us from.

Left Hand

Can you place your left hand on this page and draw around it? Then whilst talking to God, think of the difficulties that you want to give over to God. Can you write them inside the hand drawing? (If you don't want to write them why not put in initials instead?).

Then as you pray, thank God that He is your refuge and hand them to Him.

Right hand

Can you place your right hand on this page and draw around it? Thank God that you can trust Him when you are having to deal with uncertain times; why not ask Him for His help and protection? Then inside your hand drawing, why not write down what you would like to receive from Him?

#Day17

PATIENT ENDURANCE
Revelation 6:9-11

I remember as a lad reading the inspiring story of a young Russian soldier called Ivan who was arrested for being a Christian in the 1960s.[a] The atheist Communist government prevented Christians from meeting or owning Bibles, or even talking about their faith. Instead, comrades had to conform to a political ideal that actively rejected faith in God. As a soldier in the Soviet Red Army, Ivan was put to the ultimate test when he was threatened with prison when he would not deny Jesus as his Lord and Saviour. In response to his refusals to renounce his faith, Ivan was interrogated and tortured. Ivan was eventually killed adding to the number of those *"who had been slain for the word of God"* (v9).

Unfortunately Ivan's was not an isolated incident and such events are not relegated to the history books. Christians are being rejected and treated with prejudice today. Worse than that, followers of Jesus are being tortured and killed, simply because they will not change from their trust in Jesus Christ. In fact, more Christians have died for their faith in the 20th century than in the previous nineteen centuries put together. Some governments in our day have laws against any expression of Christian faith. In other places aggressive militia and terrorist groups see it fitting to round up Christians and execute them.

There is an outcry for justice from Christians today, both to governments and in prayer to the LORD. What we read in Revelation is that every person who is martyred for Jesus is registered in heaven. Each life is valuable and known to God, recognised as a sacrifice to the LORD. "Under the altar the souls of those who had been slain," (v9) reflects the place where the blood of their sacrifice rests. The blood of God's people shed through persecution is a prayer in itself. It's a cry for justice that began the day

Abel was killed by his brother in Genesis 4:10. These words were originally written to those who had seen this injustice first-hand. Their sons, daughters, wives or husbands would have been those remembered in this roll call of saints whose souls were seen under the altar.

God's response to the outcry of His people is a promise that a time is coming when the evil done against them will be properly punished. If those responsible escape an earthly trial, heaven still has a score to settle with those who persecute His saints. Revelation is written to the persecuted church. Justice in relation to those who suffer is a significant part of the build up to the day of judgement. The number of souls killed in this way is gathered up and will reach a limit where God will say "Enough!" Yet until then, there is a delay. In the meantime we read that "they were each given a white robe," which is a sign for innocence before an accusation. Although they had been judged guilty and sentenced to death on earth; in God's eyes they are blameless and worthy of honour.

So does this mean that God will fail to protect us when evil comes against us? No. Jesus is also a rescuer. The book of Acts has evidence, both of the suffering of God's people and the power of God to deliver them in miraculous ways. If we can expect persecution when we speak about Jesus, we can also expect God to send power from heaven by supernatural means, confirming His word with signs and wonders. This cry to the One who is holy and true will not be ignored; but remember, He was meant to suffer and die for us. Sometimes the same is required of us for Him.

This puts a different slant on the word "witness," which in the Greek text is "martyr." You may or may not have your life put at risk for your faith, yet sometimes we shy away from talking about Jesus with our friends in case we are insulted or rejected. This too is a form of suffering, which at times is a necessary outcome of being a follower of Jesus.

Father God. I ask that You would help me to know what to say when opportunities come my way to talk about You. Help me to endure the hardships and hurt that may result when I tell of Your love. May I not give up before I see You breaking through in people's lives. In Jesus' name.

THEY CRIED OUT *with a loud voice,* "O SOVEREIGN LORD, *holy and true,* HOW LONG BEFORE *you will judge and avenge* OUR BLOOD ON THOSE WHO *dwell on the earth?"*

#Day18

THE END

Revelation 6:12-17

I don't know if you've ever seen this, but it used to be a thing. You'd be walking down the High Street, and in amongst all the busyness would be a man wearing a sign with the words "THE END IS NIGH." He was likely to be accompanied by someone preaching in a loud voice. Naturally I made moves to avoid them at all costs. Many of their words were hard to make out, apart from some oft repeated ones such as "Sin!!" and "Judgement!!" I'm guessing that for most shoppers, these words were not incredibly appealing to hear, even with a lot of further explanation.

Whilst their message was full of truth (this world will come to an end); people can be left with the false impression that God is like an angry man who hates humankind. It's important to know that the Gospel is actually about a God who is approachable and who invites us to know Him as a good Father. He has moved heaven and earth in order to save us. Yet the fact does remain that an unstoppable day of justice is also approaching.

We read in Revelation 5 about the Lamb who looked like He had been slaughtered. This name *"the Lamb"* was first given to Jesus by John the Baptist who said *"Look the Lamb of God, who takes away the sin of the world!"* (John 1:29). Jesus, God's Son became helpless like a lamb, knowing He would be executed to save us. This act of favour towards us makes Jesus the only one fitting to open these seals that lead to judgement. He brings both love and justice. So far we have seen that the horsemen are the warning signs that precede the event where the Lamb is about to return: the end of the age. Revenge will take place against God's enemies and fair judgment towards those who have rejected Him. This great and terrible day has been graciously held back to give people a chance to make peace with God.

As John reports what he sees, we are meant to feel the magnitude of this day when the Lamb returns. John sees a shaking of nature taking place, almost like a reversal of creation. The sky *"vanished like a scroll,"* (v14) takes the idea of a scroll being rolled up after someone has finished reading it; so the earth will have had its time. The sun and moon provide balance to our days. When they are affected the world notices. A blood moon in Biblical prophecy was a sign of judgement. In fact there is a lot here that points to a day of vengeance, as darkness covers the earth and day turns to night. With the sun being black as sackcloth, a normally bright light, it also speaks of a day of mourning on the earth.

The earth is not the only thing to be affected. The heavens will also be shaken. Does *"the stars of the sky fell to earth"* mean there will be asteroids colliding with the earth? Is this why people hide themselves in caves (v15)? Jesus mentions this day in Mark 13:25. He talks about the powers in the heavens being shaken. We've seen how stars in apocalyptic language represent angels; falling ones are fallen angels. Certainly those spiritual powers who opposed God will be thrown down. There will also be a reversal of power for all earthly rulers and influencers (mountains) who have used that power for evil. All people will be brought to the same level, to face the Lamb of God who is coming.

So you might ask "Does this mean there will be a literal earthquake, black sun and blood moon?" Remember John is watching a scene unfold, that uses prophetic imagery. It expresses the physical atmosphere of events as well as deeper meanings. Rather than asteroids, it is the return of the Lamb that people run to hide from (v16), as fear becomes very real for those who don't know the LORD. The events that unfold suddenly make people realise the truth about God, because they see Him returning. Will it then be too late to do anything about it?

So how do we process all of this? We're born into a world that is focussed on shopping, sports, entertainment, leisure and enjoyment. These are all good things given to us by God to enjoy. Yet the fact is that the Creator of this world has set into motion a day and time where things such as such as sin and injustice will be dealt with. Things are about to be made new.

The words we've read speak powerfully about the rescue that God has accomplished, so that we can avoid destruction. Why not put on some Christian worship music and write out the words "Worthy is the Lamb who was slain" using the lettering below. Whilst you do this contemplate the meaning of what you are writing. With every letter you write consider the majesty of the person of Jesus and the lengths He went to save us.

Aa Bb Cc Dd
Ee Ff Gg Hh
Ii Jj Kk Ll
Mm Nn Oo Pp
Qq Rr Ss Tt
Uu Vv Ww Xx
Yy Zz

#prayerspace

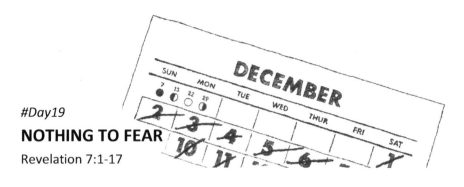

#Day19

NOTHING TO FEAR

Revelation 7:1-17

How do you feel when you've got an important day coming up in your life? It could be that you're waiting for test results, about to take a written exam or have an important interview coming up. When we don't know what a day like this will bring, it can fill us with a sense of dread or impending doom. Alternatively you might be looking forward to a sporting event, the next Marvel film or an outing with friends that makes you so excited that you can't sleep! It's only natural to wonder how key dates in our lives will turn out as we stare at them on the calendar.

Yesterday we read about the coming Day of the Lamb, this day of justice. It's only natural to ask, "If this happens in my lifetime, what will happen to me?" As you read this chapter, keep in mind that these are still the events unfolding from the sixth seal of the previous chapter, which began with a great earthquake. But it's like someone has hit the rewind button, back to that great earthquake to show us what will happen to God's people on that day. The four angels stand at the four corners of the earth about to release the disturbances that start at the beginning of seal six.

When we read a book, we expect the events to be arranged in time order. If they aren't, we assume we'll be clearly told that what we're reading happens three days earlier or something like that. With Revelation this does not happen. "After this I saw," doesn't mean "this will happen next," but rather that John saw it next in his vision. However, there are clues which help us figure out when there's a flashback moment.

A big clue is that the seventh seal hasn't been opened yet![a] We've had the opening action scene, which sees a big impact on the world, the Day the Lamb returns. Now if you are a follower of Jesus, this is an answer to the question "What will happen to me on that day?" Before the angels release the winds that bring harm to the earth, everything stops: *"Do not harm the land or the sea or the trees until we put a seal on the foreheads of the servants of our God"* (v3). The urgent command is given to spare God's people the dread of Judgement Day. They must be sealed, protected from being judged guilty, found innocent and kept from harm. This seal, visible in heaven reveals God's ownership and protection of us.

"Will I be in that number?" we ask. This number (144,000) rather than being a limited quantity of people actually reflects the perfect identity of God's chosen people. What started with just twelve tribes and twelve disciples has multiplied into a great number. What's 12 x 12? You do the Maths! The early church (both Jews and non Jews), identified as being part of the twelve tribes, as are all of those who follow Jesus the Messiah (James 1:1). This was a continuation of the ancestral identity which now included people who are not Jews, people from every corner of the world. The first tribe listed reflects this, since the Messiah comes from the tribe of Judah (v5). As we read on, we are reassured that there is room in heaven for all who will follow Jesus, "After this I looked, and there before me was a great multitude that no one could count" (v9).

It's clear from what the elder says that more days of persecution lie ahead *"These are they who have come out of the great tribulation"* (v14). However, this picture of the multitude tells also of a joy set before us, of a time to come where the sufferings of the church will have come to an end. The excitement of heaven releases a song from our hearts, thankful that God's saving plan has been accomplished. It's a time of celebration that enjoys God's closeness, recognising what it cost Him to save us.

As well as suffering in this life, those who know and follow Jesus also have a hope that will not prove false. He has sealed you and me with the Holy Spirit. He will help you. You will not be harmed on the Day of Judgment. There is nothing to fear on that day. Rather it is a day to look forward to, of incredible excitement where we will meet the LORD in heaven and see Him face to face. "But what about my friends?? They don't know Jesus!" you might ask. The next page will help you to share your faith with them.

TELLING OTHERS ABOUT YOUR FAITH

Lord. Please put someone on my heart who I can share my faith with.

Write the name, or draw a picture of the person Jesus wants you to tell about Him

Lord please show them who You are

What experiences of You can I share with them?

Lord. What do they need to hear today?

Lord help me to love and not judge
Lord what do you love about this person?

Please show me what I can invite them to.

Lord please help them through their tough times

FIRE FALLING
Revelation 8:1-5

I don't know if you've experienced travelling on the London Underground "Tube" during the working week. There appears to be an unwritten rule which everyone seems to know about, where talking to or smiling at other passengers is not the thing to do. The general expectation is that you ignore everyone else and respect people's private space.

So I was sitting in a Tube train travelling through London, when a man wearing a suit, carrying a briefcase and umbrella got on. There were no seats available, so he stood in a space in front of where I was sitting. His hands were already full, but somehow managed to pull out a newspaper and began reading. As the doors closed, I couldn't help but notice that the man wasn't holding on to anything. I kept watching, sure of what would occur; although I couldn't believe it was actually going to happen.

Well it did. As the train lurched into its forward momentum, the man fell back, like a tree cut by a lumberjack. Even more surprising was that I was going to do something about it. Quickly and skilfully, I leapt into action, catching the man in time to save him from hitting the floor! Helping him back to his feet I said (to help ease the embarrassment), "These trains really can take you by surprise!" and the man? He didn't say a word!

Why did I even think of catching the man? It's funny, but a few days before I had attended a Pentecostal prayer meeting. My friends and I had been picked out to catch people as they fell, overwhelmed by the power of the Holy Spirit! The church had gathered to ask the Lord to move powerfully in London in preparation for a mission and things got powerful!

The accounts of the New Testament church at prayer in Acts 4:29-31 tell us what they prayed for as they faced persecution. They prayed for God to help them speak for Him and to intervene in supernatural ways as a signpost to others that God was real. God immediately answered, shaking the place they were in and filling them afresh with the presence and power of the Holy Spirit. In the bit we read today in Revelation 8:1-5, it shows the significance of the prayers of God's people before God's throne. The sound of continual worship stops suddenly as the prayers of all of God's people are brought before God. The censer is a large bowl carrying prayers on behalf of others, asking for God's purposes to come to pass. These appear to be added to the prayers of the martyrs, as they are said to be from all of God's people. What do you ask for when you pray for others? Often we ask for God to reveal Himself to those we love.

Do you notice here that our prayers get the attention of God? They aren't just put on God's "to do" list, left for another time. They are the focus of His full attention. His angels respond immediately to His wishes. Some translations use the word "hurled" as if the angel throws the fire to the earth in judgment, but others use the more likely "cast" like a net. What is going on here? In response to the prayers of His people, God sends the fire of His Spirit which you can read about in Acts 2. If you read on to Acts 2:17-21, you will see that it talks about what will follow such an event *"The sun will be turned to darkness and the moon to blood"* (Acts 2:20). Remember reading that before? (Rev. 6:12). This scene that John sees in His vision is another rewind moment. It reflects events in history where God answers the prayers of His people and moves in power.

Other language we've seen before is of "flashes of lightning, rumblings and peals of thunder" (Rev. 4:5) which represents the powerful presence of God. Like a net, this fire of God is cast over the earth, shaking its foundations as God miraculously reveals Himself to humankind. This is something God wants to do, to speak His words, to heal, to set people free and for His kingdom to come in power on the earth.

If you have a passion for God to come close and overwhelm people by the power of the Holy Spirit, this will encourage you to pray and not give up! Go after God, as your prayers are receiving His full attention in heaven!

Lord. Send revival, start with me.

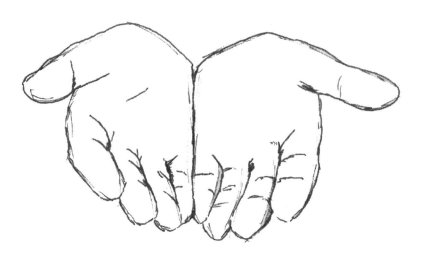

Father God. Please show me what
you want to change in my life.

I surrender my life to you, so that
you can work your wonders
through me.

Father God. This is what I surrender to you...

#Day21

SOUNDING THE ALARM

Revelation 8:6-9

Ever gone away for a weekend with your youth group? I've often taken groups away on residential trips for fun times together. Once we stayed at a location by the mountains of Mourne. The site was purpose built, with four to a room and en suite facilities. Sounds like the ideal set up? It was, until the second night of our stay. It reached 1:30 in the morning, all was finally quiet. I could think of getting some much needed sleep.

Half an hour after drifting off to sleep I was awoken suddenly by the sound of a loud siren. A fire alarm was going off in our building. Waking up somewhat disorientated I leapt out of bed, which is not easy when you're in the top bunk! Up before the other leader in the room could say "What's that noise?" I searched blindly for the light switch. Locating my jeans, I rushed out into the common room area to find people emerging from their rooms. Folks were not keen to be facing the freezing conditions outside in their pyjamas. Thankfully the alarm stopped.

After checking everything was okay, we all went back to bed. Now back in the top bunk, like an alarm clock on snooze, off went the fire alarm again! Then, forty minutes after it had stopped we were up again, back in the common room. This time teddy bears had also been woken up. Despite reassurances from the night manager, none of us were confident of a good night's sleep. As people returned to bed, some of the lads decided it would be a fun time to prank the girls. Two more alarms were to follow. In ancient times they used trumpets to alert people when there was a fire, but I don't expect any randomly sounded at the smell of a bit of toast.

Did you notice that yesterday's reading showed the scroll with its seven seals having been fully opened? We said that the seals opened are like birth pains, signposting the return of Jesus. Now we have seven trumpets. The first four trumpets are sounded as warning sirens, declaring that creation is coming to an end. Again these are a "rewind moment" sharing the time span of the four horsemen in seals one to four. If the seals are signposts, then the trumpets are alarm bells. These are a wakeup call of a Day of Judgment to come, in the hope that people will turn back to God for safety. Are these trumpets releasing judgment on the earth? Days of woe will come at the sound of the fifth trumpet, what then do we learn before this takes place?

The first two trumpets are aimed at the earth. The use of a fraction here is not meant to be a statistic. "A third" represents limited disasters, rather than simultaneous chaos in every nation. We hear of disasters on the news in distant locations. It is enough to make the world take notice. The word "burned up" (v7) brings to mind uncontrollable forest fires causing widespread destruction and melting ice caps. Although we will do our best to reverse the damage done to this world, these are problems that cause us to see how much we really depend on God to sustain the earth.

The *"mountain thrown into the sea"* of the second trumpet (v8), represents the fall of empires both military and financial, being destroyed or becoming bankrupt. Wars and economic downturns have a massive effect, like a stone dropped into water causes many ripples outwards; a mountain by proportion impacts many lives with hard times. In ancient times trade depended on the transport of goods by ships. We place our trust in governments and large corporations, but even these cannot give us the security we need. As the rulers that this world relies on are removed, like an alarm bell directing people to the only safe way out, these trumpets warn of judgment to come and of where to find safety. These are things *"which must take place"* (Rev 4:1), as the world and all of creation comes to an end.

Father God. I can see that you are the One who sustains all things. You are in charge. You make sure that this, Your world, has what it needs. May I continue to rely on You in the tough times and the good times. Thank You that You are loving and faithful to all who will trust in You. In Jesus' name!

THE FIRST ANGEL

blew his trumpet, and there followed hail

AND FIRE MIXED WITH BLOOD

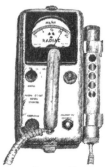

DARKNESS FALLS

Revelation 8:10-13

Shock news can be something quite unforgettable. Maybe you remember what you were doing when you heard your school was to be closed in the wake of the COVID 19 virus? Moments like these stick in our memories, our minds instantly recalling where we were when we heard the news. I remember seeing the news report of Princess Diana's fatal car crash on a Sunday morning. I first heard of the 9/11 terrorist plane attacks over the radio whilst shopping for my brother Andy's birthday card.

In 1986 I recall seeing the pictures on the news of the explosion at the Chernobyl nuclear reactor in Ukraine. Clouds of radioactive material were sent spewing up into the sky and continued to burn for 10 days. The disaster contaminated much of the surrounding area, lakes and rivers, killing some instantly and poisoning others. Actually, this disaster has been linked to the reading you have read today in Revelation! Following the catastrophe, a rumour began to spread through the Soviet Union that the events of the Chernobyl disaster were spoken about in Revelation 8:10-11: *"...a great star fell from heaven, blazing like a torch, and it fell on a third of the rivers and on the springs of water. The name of the star is Wormwood. A third of the waters turned bitter, and many people died from the waters that had become bitter."*

At the time if you were to look up the word "Chernobyl" in the Russian dictionary, one of its references would have been to the bitter herb called "wormwood." Many across the Soviet Union began to ask if Revelation linked the events of the third trumpet to the nuclear disaster where the name "Wormwood" is synonymous with Chernobyl.

Biblical prophecy can be fulfilled in more than one way. What is predicted may come to pass in the era in which it was spoken as well as being fulfilled with uncanny accuracy in the distant future. Many of the prophecies about the Messiah do this. The trumpets of Revelation relate to the time period after Jesus' resurrection, they speak of numerous events of a similar kind throughout history. Perhaps the Lord was using this incident to speak to the Soviet people of this end time reality, in order to save many souls. It may be that events in history are brought to mind that reflect the "feel" of Revelation occurrences. A word of caution though! Identifying current events or those of the past can be of value; but using Revelation to predict detailed future events, naming people or places is ill-advised! (Unless it's the return of the Lord Jesus to the earth!).

The attention of the third and fourth trumpets is turned toward the heavens, meaning the spiritual realm rather than heaven itself. In apocalyptic language a falling star represents an evil angelic power which has been influencing those on the earth and is now brought down. Its downfall, though taking place in the heavenly realm also has an impact of fury on the people of the earth. Does it poison the minds of people, making them bitter towards God? Perhaps people see it as a torch, looking to it to be a guide in the dark (v10)? A river brings life; instead here its result is a bitter attitude that causes people to perish.

Do you remember the sixth seal mentioning the sun, moon and stars being affected? This ominous darkness over the earth is indeed that which precedes the Day of the Lamb of seal six. How can *"a third of the night"* (v12) be without light? Isn't night-time normally dark? It tells of dark times ahead, of an increase of evil on the earth as the time for the Lord's return approaches. The words of the eagle declare that things are about to get real dark (v13), as three "woes" are pronounced in judgment. This judgment to come is directed towards *"those who dwell on the earth"* (v13), meaning the people of the earth who have rejected God; now God is about to reject them.

With these warning trumpets we see natural catastrophes, the downfall of empires and the fall of spiritual powers alerting us to the judgement to come. God's free gift of life is still on offer, but not for much longer...

God is our refuge and strength, an ever present help in times of trouble

Psalm 46:1

Be still and know
that I am God
Psalm 46:10

#Day23
HORDES OF HELL
Revelation 9:1-12

I don't know if you are familiar with the films "The Hobbit" and "The Lord of the Rings"? Set in the peaceful land of Middle-Earth, a threat to peace emerges across the region as secret preparations of evil are underway. A vast army of Orcs and Goblins are being mobilised, spawned in the depths of underground tunnels. Darkness begins to cover the land as these creatures that are bred to kill and plunder grow large in number. When the order is given for this army to march out in battle, you can almost feel the fear of those who will have to stand and face them.

The bit we read in Revelation today brings to mind scenes a bit like this. It's scary. The question that immediately comes to mind is: "Is this world actually going to be taken over by an army of giant locust creatures??" You'll be pleased to hear that the answer is "no." However this doesn't mean that nothing is going to happen either! These scary images represent the inescapable release of a horde of evil that will attack those who are not followers of Jesus.

Again we see an evil angel *"a star fallen from heaven"* (v1) active and given permission to harm the earth. He is appropriately named *"Apollyon"* (v11) which means "destroyer." It's not hard to guess what is about to follow. Given access to the place where demonic powers have been kept captive, the destroyer opens this abyss, releasing demons to wreak havoc as they influence the people of the earth. A horde of dark spiritual powers emerge; appearing as locusts, because they move together in great numbers devouring everything in their path. A swarm of locusts is an unstoppable force of nature that leaves a trail of destruction in its wake. An approaching swarm turns the sky dark changing the atmosphere to one of fear and darkness. Much of Revelation is written so that we get a feel of the atmosphere of events taking place. Sometimes abstract concepts of the unseen spiritual realm are best communicated with surreal picture language. Yet what we are reading is not poetic fantasy. John sees a warning of what is to come. Demonic forces are very real and are at work in our world today. The book of Acts reports, *"Crowds gathered... bringing their sick and those tormented by impure spirits"* (Acts 5:16 - NIV). Yet this first "woe" introduces us to a whole other level of darkness that the world has not seen before.

They will come *"like horses prepared for battle"* (v7) with their mission to attack, to steal from and to destroy lives. Unlike real locusts which normally feed on vegetation and leave humans alone, these fallen angels are told *"not to harm the grass of the earth or any plant or tree"* (v4). Instead they focus solely humans alone! However, those who love and follow Jesus, with the seal of the Holy Spirit are not to be targeted. Do you notice that this uses the same language of the sixth seal? (Rev 7:3). These events take place as the Day of Judgment draws near.

How will these demonic powers appear? How will they torment people? Having *"faces that resembled human faces"* (v7), we can expect evil to control humans, causing much of this misery. This torment is described as having *"stings like scorpions"* (v10) that hurt. Hardships that come because of evil in the hearts of leaders will bring about both mental and emotional anguish. Events such as these will test the resources of the most well equipped nations. This could threaten to steal any hope in life.

Not meant to be an exact amount of time, *"Five months"* (v5) is actually the approximate life span of a locust. The time period of this attack is limited. What is taking place is a warning. For those that desire to live in a place without God, this is a taste of what our world would be like without the Lord. We've been shown the scenes of natural disasters, financial crashes, wars and global insecurity. Here people will witness the reality of a place where evil is allowed to do what it wants. God is not responsible for the pain and torment of this world. This is what the followers of Jesus will be rescued from for all eternity! What better motivation to tell others of the goodness of God?

THEY WERE TOLD NOT
to harm the grass of
THE EARTH OR
any green
PLANT OR ANY TREE,
but only
THOSE PEOPLE
who do not have
THE SEAL OF GOD ON
their foreheads.

#Day24
A FINAL CALL
Revelation 9:13-21

How good are you at responding to warnings? Let's see then... Say you're searching for something online; it could be a funny story, a free download, or some key information that completes your homework. You've spent ages trawling through websites, blogs and online shops, all of which have led to one dead end after another. Then finally, your list of searches comes up with a link to what you've been looking for. You click on the link, but before you can gain access to the website, a warning appears that this is not a trusted site. Do you click?

It's tricky, because so much of our lives contain warnings. From food packaging with information about allergies, to sports shoes with mini sachets warning us not to eat them; our brains are constantly processing warning levels. Some warnings need our immediate attention but are not life-threatening, such as battery level indicators. Other warnings actually tell us about a risk to life, like road traffic signs or that sense of fear we get when climbing a tall ladder. We know that warnings are important; but as we'll see today, some we ignore at our peril.

As we read about the sixth trumpet sounded by an angel, a final warning is being sounded. It's of a similar nature to that given to the Egyptian Pharaoh who refused to let the Hebrew slaves go in Exodus 11. The last of the historic plagues displayed to a stubborn Pharaoh was the warning of death. This was the crucial moment where God set His people free.

After showing the torture of what a world without God would look like, things are about to get worse. From the altar (the place of justice and divine power), an instruction is given to four angels (Rev 9:14), who have been held, prepared for this very moment. They release what looks like an army on horseback wearing hellish armour, causing death to a third of humankind. Jesus talks about this moment in Matthew 24:37-41, where *"Two men will be in a field; one will be taken and the other left"* (Matthew 24:40). Those without the seal of God are at risk of being taken and killed, whilst God's people remain protected on the earth.

Why such destruction? You might ask. Is this not too much? The answer is that the warning level is as high as it goes. Much like the time had come for the Hebrew slaves to be released from Egypt, this vision that John sees tells us that there is no more time left. The situation is desperate. This is not a warning people can afford to ignore.

What are the people of the earth doing in response to these terrible tragedies? They are *"worshipping demons and idols of gold and silver and bronze and stone,"* v20. The believers who first heard these words would have recognised the connection between the worship of Roman gods and unholy supernatural entities called demons. Connecting with the spiritual realm of the demonic is a step towards evil. It is darkness instead of light. These are lies instead of the truth. Imagine you are God and you can see people being lied to, tricked by false powers and led away from eternal life. You would call it out as fake too! Some people are of the view that all spiritual paths lead to God; that they are just expressed differently. Here God does not give us this option. Jesus makes Christianity stand out from all the rest by saying *"I am the way, and the truth, and the life. No one comes to (God) the Father except through me"* (John 14:6).

It's plain to see that this choice makes all the difference. Who will you put your faith in? If you put your faith in God, He will require something of you which the people of the world failed to do. They *"did not repent"* (v20). It's not enough for us to just believe if we don't then put it into practice. By faith we tell God we're sorry for what we have done wrong, and crucially, we decide to turn away from going after those things in life. Instead we turn our lives towards God, discovering what He is like, honouring Him with the way we live our lives and putting Him first. In response God gives us His Spirit, as a seal protecting us, to live inside us, guiding us in all truth and being with us right through into eternal life.

THE SIXTH ANGEL
blew his trumpet,
AND I HEARD A VOICE
from the four horns of
THE GOLDEN ALTAR BEFORE GOD

#Day25

THE MYSTERY

Revelation 10:1-11

I remember the day I was queueing in a banking hall, waiting to pay in some money. It had been an ordinary day, nothing particularly special going on, when I felt God speak to me. I was third in line from being served, when God drew my attention to one of the cashiers and the thought flashed through my mind, "Tell her 'Your faith in God will be rewarded.'" Immediately I tried to forget it; but as a thousand excuses came to mind, I could tell it was one of those moments where God was really speaking. But what would happen if a different cashier called me over? Would I queue up again? Now that just looks suspicious. Not what you want in a bank. What if this lady was an atheist? Maybe that could be a good thing? What if she got really upset? Not such a good thing.

As I got to the front of the queue, I asked myself what I would actually say. "Do I just say those exact words? Do I ask her about her life first? What if I trip over my words? What if she thinks I'm trying to chat her up?" Then in timely fashion, the lady called me over. I looked to see if there were any clues to tell if she was a Christian or not. She was not wearing a cross. Did she have a name badge? A name like "Blessing" might suggest she had Christian parents! There were no name badges in sight. So I simply said "I don't know if you are a Christian or not..." Immediately she looked up at me, "Yes!" she said excitedly. I looked her in the eye and said, "I felt God say to me that your faith in Him will be rewarded." Her face lit up and as she told me that "it meant so much" to her. I left the bank super happy that for that special moment and vowed never to ignore God again!

There's an element of mystery in the ways God works which is clarified in Revelation. We see evidence that God is fully in charge, causing what must happen at the right moment. It's easy to look at today's reading and think

106

that nothing much is happening, but it's quite the opposite.

A mighty angel appears with proportions larger than Godzilla! He appears with every indication that he has been in the presence of God. Wrapped in a cloud, he brings to mind the times when God has appeared to His people. With a rainbow over his head he bears God's promises. The angel's face is glowing having seen the LORD face to face. With legs like pillars of fire he stands as a protector of God's people, ready to guide in God's purposes. He fully represents God as he calls out *"like a lion roaring"* (v3) with God's kingly authority. Then seven thunders are sounded as powerful words of God are spoken over all of creation. No one likes to be the wrong side of a secret. What are these words?

Like the seven seals and seven trumpets, the seven thunders are likely to relate to the same time span of events. The thunders released are words spoken which communicate something of the power and mystery of God's ways to the people on earth. It is something John needs to know and which we don't. God has words for John to bring to the earth. So to mark this moment John is given a scroll to eat. Eating the scroll represents the sweet goodness of the words he is given which bring the mystery of the Good News of Jesus to the people. These words are not to condemn but to call forth life in people to see the reality of God. Yet by offering life and rescue from death, eating the scroll gives John a stomach ache. There are those who will stubbornly reject this message, and will bitterly experience the judgment to come.

As the angel trumpets sound, we see hardships happening on the earth with demonic forces causing havoc. We can be tempted to wonder if everything has got out of hand. The one who created the heavens, earth and sea and everything in it has decreed that some things must take place. He has also spoken out His words of life over creation. God continues to speak out His words of life through His people in these end times.

Father God. I love Your words of life. I thank You that You want to use me to speak Your words to people today. May I prophesy your goodness to those around me, watching You transform their lives. In Jesus name!

THANKS

THINGS GOD HAS DONE

GOD YOU ARE

in my life you have...

i trust that you are:

what i love about you is

HELP ME WITH...

I devote this to You:

#Day26

SAVED

Revelation 11:1-14

One of the greatest victories of all time was forged during a moment of utter defeat. In 1940 the Allied armies of Britain, France and Belgium were in retreat. Pushed back by German forces, they were trapped on the beaches of Dunkirk. As Allied forces awaited evacuation they had nowhere to go. This gave German planes the advantage, attacking the helpless soldiers. In response to the desperate situation, all boat owners with craft suitable for shallow waters were called upon to assist in the mass evacuation of troops alongside naval vessels. As a result over 338,000 troops were safely evacuated from Dunkirk to the sound of much celebration. What was considered certain defeat was turned around to become an incredible rescue, leading ultimately to victory. What we read in Revelation was first sent to a church facing a tough battle against overwhelming odds. Pushed back on every side, was evacuation possible?

The scene is first set where John is handed a rod to *"measure the temple of God and the altar and those who worship there"* (v1). As an act that speaks about the future, John's measuring represents the preparation being made for the coming of God's kingdom to be restored on the earth. He surveys the inner area of the temple, as if making ready God's people for what is to come. As John works out the dimensions, he's setting up a barrier around the LORD's people to protect them from perishing, during a tough time where the things of God are disrespected by unbelievers.

The next picture is like someone has used a camera lens to zoom out from the detail to remind us of the bigger picture. It brings together the worlds of the Old and New Testament, showing how the people of God have taken their stand through the ages. At the same time it is focused on a period of time known as 1,260 days (the time between Jesus's ascension and His return), to tell of what is to come for God's people.[a]

Who are the two witnesses? The angel says, *"These are the two olive trees and the two lampstands..."* (v4). Olive trees were linked to Temple worship in the Old Testament, producing oil which was used to keep the lampstands burning. We know from Revelation 1:20 that the lampstands are the church, standing as the light of God's inspired word for the world to see. The two witnesses represent the testimony of God's people from both Old and New Testament that has accumulated through the ages and is now spoken by the church.[b] The prophetic words of the Messiah are more important than ever as they confirm that Jesus is God's Son.

As the church (displayed by two witnesses) speaks out the purposes of God and of the end, it faces opposition. It's a bitter-sweet message. The sackcloth they wear shows that these witnesses are not there to judge, but to warn of the Day of Judgment to come. It's also a sign of sadness, calling people to genuine sorrow for their wrong doing. When we tell of God's purposes we are indeed prophesying His will for the earth. Even though it's a desperate message of love, it's not always one that people are tuned into because of so many other things vying for their attention. God will confirm His words with signs and wonders, with power over creation to set Satan's captives free. Those who attack the church are considered God's enemies and will be justly dealt with (v5). These signs show that God has sent His church, otherwise many people won't believe.

The picture John is given tells of a time of persecution that the church will endure, which leads to what looks like a crushing defeat. The people of the earth see this defeat and celebrate; but they are forgetting what happened to the author of our faith! A resurrection takes place that makes the world sit up and take notice. Just as Jesus rose from the dead, His followers do the same thing! *"Then they heard a loud voice from heaven saying to them "Come up here!"* (v12) tells of the moment the Lord appears in the sky as He returns for His church.

Do you ever feel downtrodden or defeated? You are in good company! What you are going through is not the end. Trust the One who does the miraculous and resurrects the dead. These words of Revelation are to encourage those in defeat; that victory is still on the table!

BUT AFTER THREE AND A HALF DAYS

a breath of life from

GOD ENTERED THEM,

and they stood up on their feet

#Day27

AGREEMENTS

Revelation 11:15-19

Did you ever make trades when you were in junior school? Maybe it was Pokémon cards, friendship bracelets or just a lunch-time snack; where on the basis of an agreement a swap was made. I remember my friends and I being into unique pull-back cars. I had this super stylish Renault 5 with blue metallic paintwork. One of my friends desperately wanted it, but all he had was this orange dune buggy that I didn't like at all. There was no chance of a trade! That was until another friend came along with a cool Knight Rider car from a TV show that I was a big fan of. It turned out that he really wanted the orange dune buggy, but not my car.

My friends came up with an idea. I could swap my Renault 5 for the dune buggy, and then the dune buggy for the Knight Rider! It was agreed! The very next day I did the swap for the orange dune buggy. Unfortunately, the guy with the Knight Rider car turned up without the car. He wasn't so sure about the deal any more, which left me stuck with a car I hated!

What we read today in Revelation throws light on this question: "Why does God allow Satan to do the things he does on the earth?" God is more powerful than all evil. Why doesn't God just zzap him?? Problem solved? Ummm... if only it were that simple! The answer to this question is that we as a human race made an agreement which invited evil into this world.

The book of Genesis tells how God created the world and that it was good and without any evil. The vast garden that surrounded Adam and Eve had many trees. There was just one tree which God told them they were not permitted to eat from. This was the tree of the knowledge of good and evil. Adam and Eve already knew what good was, they experienced it every day. Essentially God was saying "Don't eat the fruit from this tree because if you do, you'll discover what evil is. You will experience evil and invite it into this world." God wanted humankind to only experience what was good. Unfortunately, as we have done so many times too, Adam and Eve chose to listen to Satan's lies instead of obeying God. Eating the fruit became like an agreement, giving Satan a legal right to affect the earth.

Jesus' sacrifice was God's way of breaking the power of that agreement and forging a new one. What we read in Revelation is how the world is seeing out the consequences of the agreement that humanity made with the enemy, as God's plans come into effect for a new world without any evil. With this idea of agreements in mind, the words *"for you have begun to reign"* (v17) make more sense. I'm sure you were wondering: "Hasn't God always been reigning?" Yes. God is King over everything, including our world. He has always been in charge. There is no power greater than He. Yet the kingdom of darkness has tried to establish a place on the earth. Jesus called the devil *"The ruler of this world"* (John 12:31). Evil is present, not as powerful as God, but able to cause havoc nonetheless. The Lamb Jesus Christ and His sacrifice has broken the hold that the enemy has on the earth, replacing it with an agreement of His own. So humankind needs to take Jesus up on His offer of life whilst it still stands!

So God reigns as King. Described as the One "who was, and is," but the words "who is to come" are missing (v17). This is because we are seeing the time when the LORD's kingdom has come. We're reading about the future moment when He returns to reign unchallenged, having taken the earth back by force. *"The Kingdom of the world has become the Kingdom of our Lord and of His Christ,"* tells of the earth finally being rid of evil.

Under the influence of evil, the nations have raged against God; but now all will be made accountable. For now there is a battle, a clash of kingdoms; where God's kingdom is breaking through and disarming the kingdom of darkness. It's exciting to know that we as God's people have a part to play in His kingdom, to destroy the works of the enemy.

Lord Jesus. You are not only the Lord of heaven, but the Lord of earth too. Please use me to "Let Your Kingdom come," on this earth, bringing Your love and power to the lives of those who have been harmed by the enemy.

we give thanks to you,

LORD GOD ALMIGHTY, WHO IS AND WHO WAS,

for you have taken your

GREAT POWER AND BEGUN TO REIGN.

#Day28

SIGNS

Revelation 12:1-6

Did you ever have a part to play in a Christmas Nativity production? Were you Mary or Joseph? An angel, sheep or a donkey?! I've been in a few, but one part I have never played is a wise man. Maybe I had the wrong look! Ah the wise men; the bearers of precious gifts, who spot the star in the east. Immediately they drop everything and go rushing off after it. Or do they? The Bible tells us they arrive in Bethlehem well after the birth, entering a house that Mary and Joseph are living in. The star is thought to have appeared in the sky the moment Jesus came to be in Mary's womb. That's nine months to get from Babylon to Bethlehem! Maybe they spent a lot of time studying and discussing the star first (or shopping for gifts!). We assume that it was in their job description as wise men to chase after stars. To observe stars yes. To follow after them? Not so much. So what was it that made them eventually decide to journey far to the place of Bethlehem? It wasn't simply one star that persuaded them, but a number of constellations together telling the story of the birth of a king.

John talks of a *"great sign"* appearing in heaven (v1). Researchers have said that it's possible this scene we read about in Revelation 12:1-6 was observed by the wise men in the constellations of the night sky.[a] A woman covered by the sun, with the moon at her feet, crowned with stars near a lion constellation with a serpent lurking nearby. The wise men said *"We saw the star in the east"* (Matthew 2:2). These constellations rise from the east, up into the sky by day for the wise men to follow westward as they set by night. Is this a sign of the Lord, written in the cosmos timed perfectly to coincide with the birth of the Messiah?

We read in Revelation another rewind moment; a big picture covering the time of Jesus's birth. The woman is Israel. Jesus was born a Jew. She also represents the Christian church that includes us as Jesus's followers today. The crown the woman wears shows her identity with each star being one of the twelve tribes of Israel. She is clothed in the sun, a picture of being right before God. And the moon? Jewish days were viewed as beginning in the evening. The moon here shows of a new thing about to take place.

Like the appearance of an arch enemy in a film, there is also a spiritual enemy seen to be at work in John's vision. This enemy is hoping to stop the Son of God from achieving His purpose on the earth. The great dragon is the serpent, the devil. His size reflects the amount of destruction he will cause. Why does he have seven crowns? They are his influence over the earthly kings and rulers throughout the world, like King Herod. A horn is a picture of strength. To have ten horns shows the power and influence that the devil had, getting a portion of angels from heaven to side with him: *"His tail swept down a third of the stars of heaven"* (v4).

Why didn't the wise men arrive on time for the birth of Christ? When Herod hears that the wise men say the baby will one day be a ruler, like the dragon he waits, intent on murder. In Matthew 2:16-18, he orders the death of all boys in Bethlehem, two years old and younger in an effort to kill Jesus. Thankfully the late arrival of the wise men allows Mary and Joseph time to be prepared for their escape to Egypt. After Jesus has successfully returned to heaven, having achieved victory over death and hell, the anger of the dragon is then turned towards Christ's followers. It appears to us such a mystery why some hate Christians with such venom. This explains it. The dragon is the driving force behind this persecution.

Yet God is at work! He has set aside a place of provision for the woman (us the followers of Jesus). I believe that God purposefully delayed the wise men to help provide for Mary and Joseph as they fulfilled His purposes. *"The wilderness"* is the hardships that we will face, but God promises us that He will still be working to help us in our struggles. He will miraculously make available what we need to be *"nourished"* (v6). Just because we may suffer, it does not mean God has left us. He is still with you and me. He will go ahead of us, preparing everything we need, as we follow Him through the tough times.

thanksgivings ···

ALL ABOUT GOD ·······························

WHAT GOD HAS MADE ME ···························

MY RESPONSE TO GOD ·························

.... Things I have noticed today

.... What I have discovered
                              about what God is like

.... What God has done in me

.... What I devote back to God

#Day29
TRESPASSES
Revelation 12:7-17

Why is it that no matter how large the space is, a ball game normally ends with the ball going over the fence?! As boys, my brothers and I used to play football in our garden all the time. Yet, there was always the danger of the game ending too soon after a kick too high. I'm sure you've had this, where "the wind" thwarts your best efforts at keeping the ball in your garden. The wind tended to do this a lot to our footballs.

Inevitably a ball would go into next door's garden and it was then up to one of us to go round and knock on our neighbour's door, asking for our ball back. We used to have a friendly elderly couple, who were happy enough to help us out. However, when this elderly couple moved out, our new neighbours were an argumentative bunch; you were never quite sure what mood you might catch them in. They also had a boy who liked footballs, so we didn't always get ours back.

There was however, a more risky alternative to door knocking which would also get our ball back. The person who kicked the ball could "run the gauntlet" of climbing over the fence to retrieve it. Of course climbing a fence from one side is easy enough to gauge; but getting back was not always so straight forward. I remember the panic. I was over the fence, in our neighbour's garden, treading carefully around their flowers. As I tried to orientate my brain to locate the ball, I heard one of my brothers shout "Hey there's a boy in your garden!!" On a hot summer's day with the windows open... well it was enough motivation for a person to grab the ball (or not!) and climb back over whatever stood in my way!

The truth is that I was trespassing on private property. So the shout "Trespasser!" was perfectly valid. We read today that the dragon (the devil) is thrown down from heaven. The agreement that humankind made, which handed the devil a place before God is now broken by Jesus. What was the devil doing in God's space? He was accusing people of their wrongdoings before God, demanding punishment. The war seen in heaven is won by the power of Jesus' blood standing in our defence, removing all blame. The devil no longer has a place from which to accuse us.

A while back in Revelation 5:2 we read of a scroll with seven seals that was not able to be opened. This legal document remained sealed, because no one could break the agreement over it. The pure Lamb appeared after having sacrificed His life as the only one worthy. From this moment on, like a clock ticking down, the enemy realises his time is short. The things "which must take place," (Rev 4:1) are being unveiled before our very eyes; as events through history warn of the end for God's enemies.

With the limited time that the devil has left, his anger turns upon *"those who keep the commandments of God and hold to the testimony of Jesus"* (v17). Interestingly whilst pursuing the woman, the devil attacks God's people with a flood. In response the earth helps by swallowing up the river. This shows the diminished power of the enemy over the earth. As God's people, Jesus gives us power over attacks of darkness that can impact our lives. An authority is accessed as we faithfully live for Jesus, believing in the power of His blood to disarm the enemy. Suddenly we see how to defeat the enemy through the power of prayer! As we speak out in faith, thanking God for His promises, an authority is released that can defy the laws of nature and overcome the enemy.

Ever feel accused even after you've said sorry to God? That's not the Holy Spirit! Jesus' blood has bought for us forgiveness from the guilt of all sin. The devil doesn't have any power over those who have accepted Jesus. Can you see the connection between the spiritual realm and the impact of our deeds? God is totally just, but has also made a way for us to be free.

Father God. I understand that I have trespassed against You and others, by overstepping the mark and doing wrong. Please forgive me. I thank You that Your forgiveness releases me from all accusation! In Jesus' name!

now the salvation
AND THE POWER
and the kingdom
OF OUR GOD
and the authority
OF HIS CHRIST HAVE COME,
for the accuser
OF OUR BROTHERS
and sisters has
BEEN THROWN DOWN.

#Day30

TARGETED

Revelation 13:1-10

Living under the shadow of the Empire must have been a daily challenge for Christians at the time Revelation was written. One such example took place some thirty years before in 64AD, where a fire was started which destroyed much of Rome. To deflect blame away from himself, Emperor Nero pointed the finger at Christians accusing them of the crime. Tacitus a Roman historian says that Nero rounded up followers of Jesus, falsely charging them of guilt and punishing them with *"the most fiendish tortures."*[a] In addition to the worship of Roman gods, citizens were required to honour their Emperor in a similar fashion. Those who refused to speak the words "Caesar is Lord" were in danger of severe punishment.

How could such a government have powers to unjustly treat the innocent in this way? Why single out Christians whose Lord was the most loving person that ever lived? The scene John witnesses in his vision of a beast emerging from the sea reveals something of the evil power pulling the strings of those intent on harming God's people. Helpfully, the book of Daniel (chapter 7) contains a similar picture of beasts coming from the sea. An angel explains that these are different rulers. The churches first to hear the words of Revelation would have been aware of this style of writing and understood the meanings more readily than you or I would!

The beast quite clearly represents governments and kingdoms that are against God. The picture of ten horns is the influence of ungodly kings throughout the world; its heads are world leaders in authority who wield their power unjustly. A diadem is a jewelled crown, which on the beast stands for those put into positions of high leadership by the devil, rather than by God. The names of blasphemy reflect the nature of such leaders in governments who even make claims to be gods. The description of the beast is interesting, being like a leopard, a bear and a lion. Those at the time would have been able to see how similar the power of the beast was to that of the Romans. Roman standard bearers would wear animal skins of leopard, bear or lion over their armour, showing they could conquer both the ferocious beasts of nature as well as dominate nations.

Much like Old Testament prophecy, the words of John revealed the current role of Roman rule to its hearers, as well as speaking of events to come in the future. The beast with a mortal wound is like a resurrected being. Just when one evil emperor is defeated, the beast has another ready to take his place. You'd think that the people would not continue to follow such leaders. However the pull of following the crowd is strong in a world where an anti-God mind-set is the acceptable norm. Maybe you've experienced this herd mentality at school where everyone rallies to verbally attack the Christian!

The period of time that this takes place (forty two months) is also found in Revelation 11:2, spanning from the ascension of Jesus, until the day of His return. These are the times we are living in today. The influencers may have changed, but hostility toward Christians remains. Some rulers and officials exercise open prejudice against Christians. Others block Christian gatherings and prayer from schools. There's terrorism, kidnapping and imprisonment of Christians that regularly occurs in this day and age. As opposition to their witness became increasingly hostile, it would be easy for the early Christians to think that God had abandoned them. Here, as the work of the beast is revealed, we can see the real reason for the suffering of the church. It is because the devil is using key influencers to poison minds against the followers of Jesus. With all that is going on in our lives day by day, it's easy to become distracted from our relationship with God, causing our minds to be poisoned too.

So what does God require of us in these end times in which we live? *"Here is a call for endurance and the faith of the saints"* (v10). Our time here on earth does not compare in any way to what God has in store for us in eternity! So hold fast! Strengthen yourself by meeting with Jesus and you will have faith to endure through the toughest of times.

Take time to worship God for who He is.
Write what comes to mind...

PRAISE For the ways God works

GLORY Tell of God's greatness

WISDOM His words and insight is fully trustworthy

THANKS What He has done for me

HONOUR Recognising His majesty as King

POWER The miracles that He does

STRENGTH He is a mighty God

#Day31
COUNTERFEIT
Revelation 13:11-18

If someone were to give you a fake bank note as change in a shop, do you think you would notice? What if you weren't expecting it? I used to work for a bank in London as a cashier, counting thousands of pounds of paper notes and coins every day. No one wanted to be the one who took in a dodgy one, but there was every chance it could be slipped into a wad of notes and missed when counting quickly. Even so for a cashier it would be quite embarrassing. We were so used to handling the real thing, that we should be able to tell a fake note from a mile away!

Normally the texture of the paper was all it took to stop and take a second look. A fake would feel cloth-like or too waxy. Worn, old-looking notes which were crumpled and faded always deserved a closer look. Counterfeit notes were sometimes made to look old in order to hide the lack of detail, which was clearly seen when compared with the genuine article. I remember finding one such "old note" and handing it to the head cashier, who in turn showed it to the assistant manager. "Look at the watermark!" he said, "That's not the Queen! It's one of the Ninja Turtles!"

Today we are going to see how the enemy produces fake copies of God's ways, tricking people into thinking it is God. We've been reading about the difficulties of living under the Roman Empire as a Christian; but why is it all described in such cryptic language? Every letter passed on from John's prison cell would be examined by prison officials before being sent. If John were to compose writings plainly stating that the devil was at work through Caesar, they would not get delivered and John could be executed. This is an unveiling of what is truly going on behind the scenes.

So the beast from the sea arises to support the dragon (who we know is the devil) through his control of certain Roman Emperors. This second

130

beast (from the earth) is pretending to be like the Holy Spirit. Using supernatural means, psychic and paranormal phenomena as *"great signs"* (v13), the devil causes people to believe this power is from God. We are told the beast uses these and *"deceives those who dwell on the earth"* (v14). Following fake signs tricked people into worshipping the gods of the Roman Empire. Does this mean that all supernatural occurrences are from the devil? No. For there to be a fake copy, there must also be the real thing. We read of the church doing signs and wonders in Revelation 11:5-6 where God's people display a greater power than those against them. Check out #Day20 to see how God is at work while this is going on!

How do we know if an other-worldly sign is a devil's fake or a real work of God? Signs always point us toward something. Ever heard a ghost story? Demons try to intrigue us by connecting their appearances to someone who has died. Ultimately their aim is to trick you into believing there is no heaven, hell or judgment. Supernatural signs that point in any direction other than Jesus cannot be trusted. Like fake bank notes when compared with a genuine one we can ask, "Is this building man's kingdom or God's?"

The work of the beast is to make *"the earth and its inhabitants worship the first beast"* (v12); clearly the devil's aim is to build man's kingdom under his influence. Through the ages there have been plenty of fakes claiming to speak with the authority of God, even using leadership positions in the church to oppress, harm and kill. The devil continues to influence the minds of other leaders too, enabling him to control the people. If he can deceive people into believing a particular world-view or ideology, they can be turned against the followers of Jesus.

The number 6 is one that falls short of the Bible's perfect number 7. When something is repeated three times in the Bible it's like it is being underlined or has capital letters for emphasis. The number 666 represents all the human fakes who lay claim to God's throne on the earth whilst being under the influence of the devil. It's easy to be taken in by fakes when we aren't expecting them, so we need to spend plenty of time with the genuine. Someone who regularly talks with God and reads His word will be able to spot any fake from a mile off!

then i saw another beast rising

OUT OF THE EARTH.

133

#Day32

AN OPEN HEAVEN

Revelation 14:1-5

Ever been on a car or train journey that took you through another country? On a long journey it's possible to fall asleep and not even notice that you've entered a new land. Yet when you step out of the car, it can be a strange experience. Having crossed the border, everyone has suddenly changed. They are now using a different language, a new set of laws and a transport system that can take some getting used to! The money that was in your pocket becomes unusable and everything is priced and packaged differently. We ask "How does the cost of a bar of chocolate compare with the price where I come from?"

In the bit we read today, we have a picture of God's people standing with Jesus on a place which seems to border both earth and heaven. We see the 144,000: God's people represented through the ages and continuing to this day, standing on Mount Zion. Is this the hill outside the walls of Jerusalem? King Jesus is standing with them on the earth as Messiah and ruler (see Psalm 2:6). There's a mix of both heaven and earth here with God's people *"singing a new song before the throne"* (v3), which places them in heaven, or at least in earshot of the throne.

So where are they? In heaven or on the earth? This doesn't seem to be the moment where God's people go to heaven; since we'll meet Jesus in the air rather than on a mountain. Could it be after Jesus's return, enjoying the glory of being in God's presence? But it says that "No one could learn the song except the 144,000" (v3) which indicates other living people in existence who don't follow the Lamb.

We know that whilst living on the earth we have become residents of another city, of a heavenly kingdom, because we have been redeemed. The word redeemed means to buy back (v4). This talks of how Jesus bought us back from the slavery of the devil by dying on a cross. Those of us who have received Jesus as Lord trust in the promise of heaven to come. It appears that God's people are experiencing heaven whilst being on the earth! Powerful like thunder and peaceful like an ensemble of harps, how the voice of God the Almighty contrasts to that of the beasts!

God doesn't leave us alone to face the beast without causing heaven to touch earth. As the important task of bringing the Gospel reaches its final stages, it's like God is letting His people in on a secret. A heavenly melody is heard by the LORD's people giving insight into God's ways that strengthens us on the inside. The message of the song changes the atmosphere and carries a fresh understanding of something timely about God and His plans. It impacts our thinking and encourages us in *"proclaiming the eternal gospel"* (v6).

Standing on the borders of heaven and earth we are given the task of making the land of heaven accessible to those on the earth. It's not a case of "the world's all going to pot, let's get out of here." As God's representatives, we are here to bring God's rule and to destroy the works of the devil. The power of heaven destroys things like sickness, fears and addictions. This is the rule of Jesus Christ. When we catch a glimpse of heaven it reminds us who we really are as children of God. The people of this age are seen as having little resistance to the temptations of the beast that lead them away from the Lamb; but God's people are seen here as remaining faithful to Jesus. Rather than actual writing, the names on their foreheads act like a spiritual helmet, identifying those who belong to God.

We live another way because our citizenship is in heaven (Philippians 3:20). The laws of this land are grace and truth and the language of our Father is love. Staying connected with heaven reveals that everything the beast has to offer is a trap, it is temporary, fake and leads to death. What we have in Jesus is a gift, it is eternal, true and brings life in all its fullness!

Father God. To be in Your presence is a beautiful place to be. Draw me close to You now, that I may understand more of who You are and what You are like. Let heaven come down to earth in my life! In Jesus' name!

To have some quality time with God, think about some of the things which will help you connect with Him in the best way. I've written some ideas. You might like to add your own...

#prayerspace

#Day33
JUDGMENT
Revelation 14:6-13

How satisfying is it to you when you see justice being done? How do you feel when people traffickers, terrorists and other criminals get the prison sentences they deserve? After the hurt and pain they've caused others, it's only right to know they are paying for their crimes. In a lot of films when an evil mastermind finally meets his or her end, it's normally by a horrible death. They'll not die peacefully in their sleep on a bed of soft pillows, having lived a long life. No. You can expect them to be eaten alive, have their face melted off, or be sawn in two. Why is this? It's because after all the nasty things that the villain has done, we want to see them suffer in a way that is equal to the suffering they have caused.

The part we've just read in Revelation is hard to read because it begins to talk about the events of judgment. It's important to remember that these words were first read out to people in churches who were under heavy persecution. God's people were suffering unjustly under the reign of Caesar. John, who saw these visions, would have known this only too well as he wrote down these visions from his prison cell. We know of Nero and his "most fiendish tortures;" but this wasn't just one evil mastermind responsible for such cruel injustices. Rather it was a system, an empire that was involved in these atrocities. From officials to guards and those who carried out his orders; they all had a part to play. Informers and emperor cult worshippers supported the system, with spectators ready to turn up at venues to watch those being killed for entertainment.

The picture of people tormented with fire in Revelation 14:10 would have been a very familiar one to Christians. Nero was known for lighting his garden by having Christians tied to a pole and set on fire. The theme of a repayment of justice to those who have carried out the plans of the beast is being communicated with the words *"He will be tormented with fire and sulphur in the presence of the angels and the Lamb"* (v10). It's easy to make the mistake of thinking that the scene being described here is hell; but Jesus is present. This is actually the Day of Judgment.

The word "tormented" also carries the idea of being examined. Since the deeds of those who worship the beast are not covered by the blood of Jesus, they are brought out into the open. The evil brought to light will be tested and incur the full wrath of God. God is totally fair, loving and just. He even sends His messengers calling out a desperate warning. *"Fear God and give Him glory, because the hour of His judgment has come"* (v7). This last chance for people to be rescued from hell can only be taken up before the Lamb returns, before judgment begins.

The phrase "fire and sulphur" or "burning sulphur" isn't found much in the Bible, but refers to utter destruction, rather than the idea of endless torture. The words *"the smoke of their torment will rise forever and ever"* (v11), mean that once a judgment is decided and a sentence passed, the punishment cannot be reversed. There is no chance to get out for good behaviour, to "rest in peace" in heaven at a later date. No. Only the prospect of destruction awaits those who have rejected Jesus.

I've heard some say "I can't believe in a God of judgment." Essentially that is saying "I can't believe in a God that is good." For without judgment, evil would always have a place in our world. We've seen how sin can give evil a controlling power over our lives. Remember how the world was all good until Adam and Eve came into agreement with the devil? For there to be an end to evil, judgment is one of the things which *"must take place"* (Revelation 4:1).

Although innocent, Jesus endured the horrible death fitting a villain. In love, the Lord of glory, God's Son gave himself up to be executed to pay for our crimes. We will all be judged one day. Those who have confessed their wrongs and turned to Jesus have nothing to worry about when that time comes. Our judgment has fallen on Jesus instead. We will be cleared of all blame! This is a free gift that is offered to all. The choice is ours, to face the wrath of God or to receive His mercy. Which have you chosen?

FEAR GOD AND *give him glory,* BECAUSE THE *hour of his* JUDGMENT HAS COME, *and worship him who* MADE HEAVEN AND EARTH, *the sea and the* SPRINGS OF WATER.

#prayerspace

#Day34
REAPING AND SOWING
Revelation 14:14-20

Have you ever done something that you instantly regretted? I have. I must have been about six years old at the time and I had been invited to a party. It had been a very enjoyable evening with fun, food and I believe jelly with ice cream. Now that it was time to go home, I sat on a window sill with a girl I liked waiting for mum to pick me up. It was at this moment that I decided to do something that would ruin the entire evening.

In the excitement of the moment sitting with my friend, I thought it would be funny to say a very rude poem in a loud voice. I had never said anything like it before and after what happened next, I would never say anything like it again. At that exact moment my mum arrived at the door to pick me up. Recognising my voice, the words that no child wants to hear... "Wait 'til I get you home," was enough to fill my heart with dread.

As we walked home I was now very sorry, repeating my apology beyond the point where it was annoying. I begged, promised and pleaded with mum not to tell dad, well aware of what might take place if dad found out. That night I got to bed very quickly, hoping to avoid all talk of subjects relating to parties, jelly or ice cream. When the next day came, it was as if nothing had happened! My repentant pleas had been heard. It was truly a gift of grace that I did not deserve; justice had been met by mercy!

Today we have a picture of angels with sickles and two big collections of people going on as the end of the age approaches. First John sees "one like a son of man" (v14) seated on a cloud. This is Jesus, linking His return with the events that we read of. An angel appears from *"the temple"* (v15), indicating that he is coming with instructions from God the Father. His words give Jesus the go ahead to take those who are His into heaven. When will this happen? We're told that no one knows the time of the

Lord's return, not even the Son; only the Father knows this (Matthew 24:36). So in one action, like a sickle cutting through sheaves to gather in ripe corn, the Lord Jesus will gather up those who are truly sorry for their wrongs and have turned to follow Him. Both the living and the dead will be safely brought into eternal life.

A second angel appears from the temple, coming again with a task to carry out for the Father. What is his job? His instructions are given by an angel who comes from the altar *"with authority over the fire"* (v18). In Old Testament times the altar was where an animal would be killed before God as a substitute for the wrongs a person had done. The killing of the animal showed that the action of wrong doing led to death. It would then be burned. This second group have not made the appropriate amends for their sin. They have not believed in Jesus's sacrifice to become right before God. Therefore they are to be met with the anger of God. A winepress in the Bible was used in prophetic language to communicate judgment, where the results of God's anger against wrongdoing are felt.

So, the angel is told to gather clusters of grapes to be put through the winepress of God, as punishment for sins not paid for. Interestingly like these grapes, Isaiah tells us that Jesus *"was crushed for our iniquities"* (Isaiah 53:5). This hints to us of how Jesus was the first cluster of grapes to take this punishment.[a] Through His death on a cross Jesus took God's wrath upon Himself as a punishment for sin. Isaiah says this: *"the punishment that brought us peace was upon him"* (Isaiah 53:5). Jesus' death went before everyone else, so that we may all have a chance to make peace with God. Those who have still rejected Jesus will follow on after Him into the winepress of God's judgment, before being destroyed.

Some want to accuse God of wrong for collecting up people for judgment. Yet we'll all reap what we have sown in this life. It's our wrong deeds that have separated us from God. We cannot expect entry to heaven without our sin being covered. God sent His Son to die on a cross, because it was absolutely necessary. We are prized by God. He wants us in His grain collection to be with Him forever. At great cost God has moved heaven and earth to make sure you and I can be gathered up to eternal life.

#prayerspace

"Search me, O God, and know my heart: test me and know my anxious thoughts. See if there is any offensive way in me, and lead me in the way everlasting." Psalm 139:23-24

Take a few moments to ask Jesus to search your heart, to see if there are any offensive ways that need to be dealt with.

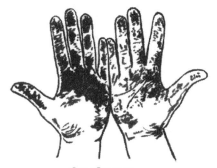

SIN STAINS

SIN DISTORTS

SIN SEPARATES

SIN GRIPS

SIN SPOILS

SIN MISSES THE MARK

In any of the spaces, feel free to write down any promises that you would like to make to God.

#Day35
SIGNPOSTED
Revelation 15:1-8

If you've ever read the account of Moses and the slaves of Egypt, you'll know it's an amazing story (Exodus chapters 7-14). Over the course of time the Hebrews living in Egypt grew in number, causing the Egyptians to mistreat and enslave them. In desperation the Hebrews cried out to God to set them free. So God chose Moses and sent him to meet with Pharaoh, telling him to let the Hebrews leave his land. Pharaoh refused. In response God instructs Moses to announce that a plague will occur, killing all the fish of the Nile if Pharaoh did not change his mind. God was going to use signs to prove to Pharaoh, the Egyptians and Hebrews that He was the only God. He would also use this opportunity to embarrass the deceptive powers behind the famed gods of Egypt.

True to His word, the Lord turns the water of the river Nile into blood. No amount of worship to the Nile gods could stop the terrible smell. Yet stubbornly Pharaoh rejects all demands to let God's people go. Then, as one plague follows another, the power of God is seen over the sky, crops, livestock and even the sun! The spiritual powers behind the gods of Egypt were revealed to be defective against the might of the LORD. In dramatic fashion, Moses and the Hebrews leave Egypt, miraculously escaping the chase of the Egyptians. God provided a safe passage through the Red Sea, before drowning the pursuing Egyptian chariots. What a moment of triumph and rescue over their slave masters! No wonder Moses breaks into song praising God for saving His people and leading them towards the Promised Land (Exodus 15:1-18).

The very purpose of a sign is for people to look at it and notice what it is pointing to. These plagues are not random events. Their purpose is to advertise the intentions of the Creator God. It's true that some people will not believe unless they witness a sign or a miracle. The plagues are that

146

sign; signs that tell of judgment to come *"for with them the wrath of God is finished"* (v1). For some, the plagues will be a final wakeup call to discover the truth. Jesus said *"when you see all these things, you know that he is near, right at the very gates"* (Matthew 24:33).

Similar in nature to the events of Exodus, the plagues also act as evidence before a promised rescue. Yet we are shown them in reverse! I'm sure you will notice that Revelation repeatedly returns to the scene of God's people, safe from harm in heaven. It's shown repeatedly, like a chorus of a song to declare that it is going to happen! Of that there is no doubt.

Much like the Hebrews cried out under the ill-treatment of their Egyptian masters, so the followers of Jesus have been crying out under the harsh treatment of their Roman oppressors. As God's people look into the sea of glass mingled with fire, it's like they are witnessing the earthly destruction from a heavenly perspective. Even when it appears that everything is falling apart around us, it's important to be mindful that the view from heaven tells of God's plan to overcome evil and bring it to a final end.

Imagine seeing anti-Christian rulers setting up oppressive regimes, which are actively prejudiced against you. Add to that people around you looking down at you because you identify as a Christian, calling you all kinds of names. On top of that events around the world are showing that there is trouble all over the earth. It could be enough to ask "Where is God in all this?" Seeing the reality of what is happening from God's perspective helps us not to lose heart and understand that God hasn't abandoned us. This kind of faith requires patient endurance, standing firm through the hardships. Those who call on the name of the Lord will be saved!

Father God. I thank You that You did not give up on this world. You refused to let evil have its way. Even though we humans invited evil into this world and it cost You the life of Your Son, You did not abandon us. Instead You provided a way of safety, which is available to all through Your Son Jesus. Lord, holy, pure and mighty, there is none like You, who acts on behalf of those who love You. Justice and truth meet love and grace through You like no other. Thank You Father, for loving me! In Jesus name!

"great and amazing are your deeds,

O LORD GOD THE ALMIGHTY!

just and true are your ways,

O KING OF THE NATIONS!

who will not fear, o lord,

AND GLORIFY YOUR NAME?

for you alone are holy.

ALL NATIONS WILL COME AND WORSHIP YOU,

for your righteous acts

HAVE BEEN REVEALED."

END GAME

Revelation 16:1-21

I have a question... Why does completing all of the levels in a video game feel like such an achievement? Should you manage such a feat, the next day might see you telling your friends at school, describing your victory in some detail. What makes this such a grand feat? It might be something to do with the challenge of the boss battles. Those super tricky monsters referred to as "bosses" stand between you and the end of that level. Any who have faced them know that it requires skill and inventiveness to beat them. The power level of a boss far exceeds those you've fought before and your average character is really no match against them. It requires no ordinary approach to fight and defeat these monsters.

Yet with every video game, worse is always to come. When the final boss appears, he's more powerful than any you've previously encountered. He's the architect of all the darkness you are fighting. If this boss is not defeated, you'll not save the world and all your efforts will be for nothing.

A bit like going through the levels of a video game, what we read today shows events moving towards the end level. The plagues poured out are aimed at those who have sided with the beast in his war against God's people. *"And harmful and painful sores came upon the people who bore the mark of the beast and worshipped its image"* (v2). You will remember back in Revelation chapter 8 we saw seven trumpets sounding the alarm as a wake-up call for those on the earth. Now we are shown the same seven events, viewed from heaven's perspective. The enemy and his followers are being targeted by plagues that go before the end rescue that God has got planned.

This is another rewind moment. Just as the first trumpet (Rev 8:7) affects the earth, so the first bowl (Rev 16:2) sees earth affected too. Now we can clearly see the target of these plagues, as God's wrath is poured out on His enemies. These bowls describe sickness, death, pollution, natural disasters, spiritual darkness, and war. Maybe events featured in the news come to mind at the mention of these things. As God's wrath is poured out, the faith of those signed up to the anti-God system is tested. Will they turn to God when they realise the system cannot save them? Like angry wasps flying out of their nest, the enemy rages with full power to war against God's people. It's like facing up to the final boss battle.

So is there going to be a final battle of Armageddon? Ummm... No. What is described is more an assembly of Armageddon! *"And they assembled them at the place that in Hebrew is called Armageddon"* (v16). If you read on, the final bowl is poured out with a voice saying *"It is done!"* (v17) and the mighty power of God is seen shaking the earth. What follows? *"Every island fled, and no mountains were to be found"* (v20). Islands are ruling nations and mountains are kingdoms. These powers will both fall away. So there is no boss battle in the end! The Lamb will return unexpectedly in power and glory. In overwhelming power He will bring about His promised rescue. After all, the power of the devil is no match for God!

The Hebrew word for Armageddon means "Mountain of Megiddo." There is a place in Israel called Megiddo where many battles have been fought. However, there is no mountain there. Rather, this is talking about a gathering of those who are battling against God. In chapter 14 we saw a different gathering, one of God's people on Mount Zion. People will make their choices and be found in one of two groups. They'll be associated with one of two mountains (kingdoms); there will be no middle ground.

So it's a strange set of circumstances. The followers of Jesus are suffering under the attack of the followers of the beast, with many being mistreated, tortured or executed. The battle rages in the heavenlies where bowls of wrath are poured out on God's enemies. The view from a worldly perspective is that the beast has the key positions of power. Yet the spiritual forces at work on behalf of the beast cannot stand where God makes His presence felt. God is working on the earth, we have not been left to battle alone. God's end game is to come.

#prayerspace

Here are some verses from Psalm 33:20-21. As you can see, there are bubbles coming from certain key words. As you talk to God, think about what these words mean and write any thoughts that come to mind in the large bubbles.

For our heart rejoices in Him, because we trust in His holy name.

#Day37

COMPROMISE?

Revelation 17:1-18

Friendship is a curious thing. It can come about when any two people are put together, it's a bond built on shared experiences and trust, and it can't be sold for money. But what if it could be sold for money? Say one of your friends is an avid gamer. He's been going on about the new VR games console for weeks and how he'll never be able to afford it. Imagine he comes to you one day and says, "Now that I'm saving up for this VR games console, you'll have to pay me if you still want to be my friend." Of course you would say "No way!" So imagine he says "Okay," and walks away. Later that day you find out that he's started offering his friendship to others at a price. Before long you are shocked to discover that people are taking up his offer and have paid him money in advance. Your friend is super-excited, as he is half-way to earning the money he needs!

A week later, things are not good. Those who have paid your friend are finding it funny to use him as a servant. He carries their bags, cleans up after them, is called names and mistreated. As time goes by you learn that your friend now has the games console. Every week he has new clothes and fancy things. Even though you've tried to talk to him, your friend now ignores you; unless of course you have some money?

In the bit we read today John is shown a vision of a woman who is attractively dressed, but all is not as it seems. Unlike the woman who gave birth to a son in chapter 12, this woman is not a righteous lady. She does not see the value of friendship with God. Having sold her friendship with God, she entices others to worship her gods; being led about by the beast who we know is the devil. John is told that this woman represents the *"great city"* of Babylon (v18). As we've said before, prophecy in the Bible was often fulfilled in the time it was spoken, as well in times to come. Here Babylon is a code word for the Roman Empire. With its anti-God mind-set it also may represent other empires to come. John is being shown the judgment that is to come upon this Empire. Many of the kings of other nations could not stand against the power of the Romans, opting to come under the control of the Empire, rather than being destroyed. Great numbers of people then had to honour the gods of the Romans.

The beast wears names that disrespect God's name, God's rule and God's authority. The woman is under its influence and follows its lead; causing leaders to make choices that make ungodly living easier for their people. Maybe you've heard the phrase "What happens in Vegas stays in Vegas"? It's not a law, but it advertised the idea that you could go and do whatever you wanted there, without worrying that someone might find out about it.

This is far removed from what God intended for His creation. The vision of this woman, attractively dressed with expensive jewellery, reveals the way the enemy works using the status of wealth to attempt to influence world leaders. The practices encouraged by the Roman Empire were influencing *"multitudes and nations"* in a negative way (v15). Why are we being shown this with such dramatic picture language? These scenes throw light on the hidden goings on of the devil's plans and why these actions must be judged. You might remember that the church in Thyatira (#Day9) had a false teacher who was leading some to make idol sacrifices; a convenient message for some of the people at Thyatira. The trade guilds there required attendance at feasts where deals were made. Yet these often involved sacrifices to idols and other inappropriate behaviour. The scene witnessed by John here reveals the disrespect that this shows towards God and how those involved are considered as siding with the beast.

So what do we do when God requires us to honour His rule and authority over our lives? There's a pull of influence today to do something "because everybody is doing it" even when it goes against what God wants. Maybe even schools teach it or governments allow it. This can be hard to resist. What about that exciting opportunity that will give us just what we want; apart from the fact that we'll have to compromise morally to get it? Whether it is a small thing or a big thing, wherever we honour Jesus as Lord of our lives, He will notice it and will honour us in return.

THEY WILL MAKE WAR ON THE LAMB,

and the lamb will conquer them,

FOR HE IS LORD OF LORDS

and king of kings,

AND THOSE WITH HIM

are called chosen

AND FAITHFUL.

EMPIRES FALL

Revelation 18:1-8

I don't know if I can talk so much about an Empire without making a Star Wars reference! Even if you've never seen the Star Wars films, you'll probably be familiar with the Death Star. This planet-sized space station resembling a moon served as the main base for the Imperial forces of Darth Vader and Emperor Palpatine. Imagine the fear of seeing the Death Star appearing in the sky. At best it meant an invasion of Storm Troopers was due any moment. At worst you could expect a powerful laser being aimed your way, able to explode your planet into millions of pieces.

Once deployed, Storm Troopers enforce the will of the Empire, with powers to arrest, torture or kill anyone of interest. Many citizens serve the Empire for a good wage or a steady job. Those who don't, stay out of trouble and do their duty. A smaller number however, opt to join the secret Rebellion. If only the Death Star could be destroyed! The Empire's influence over the people would come to an end!

Of course in the films, the destruction of the Death Star only turns out to be a partial victory. What we read today in Revelation tells of the complete destruction of the kingdom of Babylon. "Babylon" was a name often used by Old Testament prophets to represent a system of rule that chose to operate outside of the rule of God. Having replaced the Creator of the Universe with their own man-made gods, the people are misled by the beast, devoting themselves to a lie. Some kings and emperors even set up statues of themselves for people to worship. Maybe you've noticed how some celebrities do this today in pursuit of fame and fortune, leading people to worship their image?

An idol is something that has our heart's devotion. It's whatever we put first. We might not bow down to a carved statue, but our moral choices make it obvious whose ideologies we follow. Have you taken on board a set of beliefs that contradict what the Bible says? The attitude of a Babylonian mind-set is "I'm a self-made person, I make my own rules and I make my own fortune. I can even make a god that suits my preferences." This kind of thinking originates from the beast and is a shaky foundation to build your life upon. This is not the way God intended things should be.

God's word to those who will listen is clear *"Come out of Babylon, my people, lest you take part in her sins"* (v4). This isn't a call to separate ourselves from those who don't follow God, but rather to not be fooled by ideas that tempt us to take on board this self-reliant attitude. Jesus said *"...wide is the gate and broad is the road that leads to destruction, and many enter through it. But small is the gate and narrow the road that leads to life, and only a few find it"* (Matthew 7:13-14).

The danger of being influenced by the Babylonian mind-set is that it leads to destruction. The message the mighty angel brings, is exactly this. Appearing with a blazing brightness he comes shining a light on the secret lies hiding in the darkness. With words of woe he predicts the downfall of anti-God kingdoms like the Roman Empire, telling of the judgment of all nations who follow the beast. Certain destruction is predicted, as places once busy and full of activity are turned into ghost-towns.

It's easy to dismiss any thoughts that we could be following the beast or being secretly influenced by the devil. Yet as we saw yesterday, the Babylonian mind-set can appear at first to be attractive. The enemy has a way of discovering what our weaknesses are. Coming under his influence can be easier than we think. With those around us following the Babylonian way, the norm is to live without questioning if our lifestyle is just going with the flow.   God wants to shine a light on our hearts and ask us this question: "What things are currently pushing Me out of your life?"

Father God. I take this moment to consider the choices I am making and how I am spending my time; even in the last week. Help me to honestly reflect upon who it is I am following. May the living of my life show that You are my number one! In Jesus' name.

fallen, fallen is babylon the great!

#Day39
LEFT EMPTY
Revelation 18:9-24

I have a question for you... What would you be willing to do for five million pounds? To earn an amount like that might require doing something we wouldn't ordinarily want to do. Would you stay to the end of an "I'm a celebrity get me out of here" style TV show? Imagine having to sit in a pit of rats and snakes, before wading through a swamp of fish guts. Maybe you could bear 10 huntsman spiders crawling over your face, all of which you have to eat one by one? Or how would you handle an offer that required a moral compromise? Say you were offered money to steal someone else's invention idea? Would you do it? Or could you give up true love for the money? Would the offer of money be enough to make you even compromise your faith?

To have such an amount of money would be life-changing. You'd be set for life. The money could go into savings or investments for a healthy return. Your money could work for you so that you wouldn't have to. It's easy to dream of living a life of luxury and leisure. But is that what life is all about? Is the meaning of our existence here on earth to gather up enough money to live a comfy lifestyle? Surely there must be more to life than this!

In the bit we read today, we are shown three groups of people affected by the destruction of the Roman Empire (and other anti-God systems). Kings, merchants and seafarers all watch with bitter tears, shocked as the empire that supported them falls suddenly. Kings who used their influence to gain for themselves a fancy lifestyle and celebrity status have lost their riches. The merchants who came to greatness through the selling of luxuries have lost their business. Seafarers travelling far and wide to source luxury goods have lost the fame of being associated with Rome. What do those in each group have in common? They have all accepted the rule of this Babylon-style empire which rejects the reign of God. Instead they lived to satisfy themselves, chasing after luxury, wealth, glory and fame. Is it wrong to want nice things? No it isn't. However, to gain these things the merchants and others have ignored God and compromised morally. Not only have they turned away from their Creator, they have also been willing partners with those who have mistreated others. Turning a blind eye to the poor and innocent, they have served to protect their own interests, trading with the lives of human beings as slaves.

Twenty eight items of cargo are mentioned in the bit we read, in addition to the evil trade of human lives. This number of luxury goods has come from the "four corners of the earth" multiplied by seven (the number of completeness). In other words, they stand for all luxury products sourced from all over the world. The primary motivation of the kings, merchants and traders is the desire for a lifestyle filled with *"delicacies and splendours"* (v14). This has become the meaning of their lives costing them the greater glory of heaven to come. They've compromised morally, making a deal with the beast to get what they want. Unfortunately for them, their compromise will leave them empty when the empire is defeated. They will lose it all. A mighty angel is seen who took up *"a great millstone and threw it into the sea"* (v21). The sea, picture language for the place on which luxury items (including slaves) were transported, is hit with force. Its waves impact the world as a warning to all. Like a heavy rock at the bottom of the sea, this empire will never rise again.

This prediction of what is to come also serves as a warning to the people of God. Those who had become involved with ungodly trade associations to further their business would be faced with morally compromising situations. If an opportunity came our way which was to challenge the life we have in God, what decision would you or I take? Whatever it is that our heart wants, whether a relationship, a career opportunity, or even a million dollars; the question we need to ask is this: Will I be able to honour God if this opportunity came my way?

Father God. I know that this life here on earth is temporary. It can't compare in any way to the eternity of life to come. Help me never to put that at risk by doing a deal that leads me away from You. In Jesus' name.

alas! alas!
YOU GREAT CITY, YOU
mighty city, babylon!
FOR IN A SINGLE HOUR
your judgment has come.

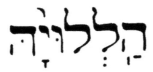

READY

Revelation 19:1-10

I have to tell you about the time when God helped me to pass an exam! It happened when I was at Bible College taking Old Testament Hebrew. I was excited to be learning Hebrew, yet at the same time it worried me. Retaining vocabulary and working out grammar made my brain ache. Of course there was also the issue of re-learning the alphabet and reading from right to left! The whole thing was a challenge to grasp. We were told that our final exam would include a Hebrew text to translate of a similar nature to those we'd be working on. One of the texts we enjoyed studying was the book of Joshua. I could translate some words, but I was certainly no expert and very aware of my limitations! I needed help. So I asked God if He would lead me to the text that was going to be in the final exam. In the meantime I continued to study hard and revise!

So one day I was reading my Bible in church, when I had a lightbulb moment! As I read I felt a sudden rush of inspiration, like God was saying to me, "This is the one!!" So I prayed some more and was convinced that this was the text. In preparation for the exam I poured all my energies into translating that text, writing out all the words and sticking them around the wall of my room. I also told my friends from the Hebrew class, so that they could benefit too. They were amazed, but unsure!

I'll never forget the moment in the exam room, as I turned over the exam paper. There staring back at me was the text I had stuck to my bedroom wall! I looked over at one of my friends to see her wide eyed. I could not hide the smile on my face! Of course this was not a short-cut to learning, but a partnership of being faithful in study, whilst relying on God for help.

The part we read today is exciting and incredible! Way back in Revelation 6:10 we saw the martyrs crying out under the bullying control of evil, asking *"How long before you judge and avenge our blood?"* The moment of rescue has come and crying out in joy they praise God for avenging their blood. Now that judgment of the corrupt deeds of the world has taken place and God's rescue has come, the heavens roar in praise.

We are then shown a picture of a wedding. Here God's people are pictured as a bride to be married and Jesus returning as the One to marry her. This picture communicates the "covenant" we have with God, an agreement where two people in relationship make promises to each other that will not be broken. Our love and faithfulness is very important to God. In Revelation 2:4 Jesus says to the Ephesian church *"you have abandoned the love you had at first."* Jesus, the Lord of glory is shown as returning and fulfilling His promise to us. He is still humbly described as the Lamb; because He made possible our rescue through His death by execution.

As Jesus returns, it is to a people who have been made ready. It's like being prepared for an exam. You can't just turn up and hope for the best! Our part in this covenant agreement requires our faithfulness to Him in the living of our lives. Yet it's not all up to our own efforts. We read that fine linen garments (righteous deeds) are given to the church to put on. The help of God is paired with our actions of obedience. We have a partnership with God, who as a good Father wants to give us all that we need. When Jesus returns unexpectedly, His invitations will have already been sent out. Earlier on in Revelation we see Jesus saying *"I stand at the door and knock"* (Rev 3:20), inviting us to a meal. The marriage supper of the Lamb uses the picture of a feast to describe how those faithful to Him will be invited to His place and taken to be with Him in heaven.

When we meet Jesus for the first time and become a follower of Him we discover that we need His help. He makes us pure because His blood pays our debt and makes us clean. Yet He doesn't stop there. He has a work of grace to do in us where He shapes our character, forms our thinking and changes our lives. We have a part to play in this. To worship Him is to submit to His reign and to want to know Him more. It's a relationship. Two people who go on a date have a very different relationship to those who are married. Marriage is founded on a covenant of love. How much more we will know the Lord when He returns and we will be with Him forever!

Take time to think about Jesus the Living One and thank Him for the confident hope we have of heaven through Him.
Why not create your own wall art like this one?

It doesn't matter if you don't manage to produce a masterpiece!
It's more important that during this time you've connected with Jesus.

#prayerspace

#Day41

OVERCOMING EVIL

Revelation 19:11-21

I wonder what it must feel like for an Olympic athlete to return home after winning a gold medal. Imagine riding home on an open top bus to see people lining the streets to celebrate the victory you have won for your nation. The years of training and self-discipline invested to earn the chance of competing for a medal place were worth it. Having overcome all the odds, you've even beaten your greatest rivals to gain the top spot. No one can take away the title of champion that you now hold.

Today we read about the returning King who achieved victory through a battle which appeared to onlookers to end in death and defeat. This King who approaches from heaven, wearing lots of crowns and riding a white horse is Jesus. He is very much alive and coming back in victory; He will reclaim the earth from the control of evil. The circumstances of His return are very different from the sorrow and humiliation He experienced when He died on the cross. We're told *"He is clothed in a robe dipped in blood"* (v13). It's His own blood; proving He is worthy to do what must be done next. It's amazing to think that God himself came to earth, to those He created and lived among us. He's so powerful that He could have ended everything with just a word. Yet He allowed those He'd created to unjustly accuse Him, to disrespect and torture Him, before unfairly executing Him.

Now He rides to conquer, no longer wearing a crown of thorns, or carrying a cross of hate; instead He returns with a victory that means no battle is necessary. To understand just who Jesus is, we are told that He is called "The Word of God" (v13). John tells us in his gospel that Jesus the Word was with God at the beginning, way back when the world was made (John 1:2). Being *"Faithful and True"* (v11) means that His words and actions match up. A few verses earlier we read *"The testimony of Jesus is the Spirit of prophecy."* (v10) The reports of what Jesus did are true. His power lives, being fulfilled throughout every generation. We've already discovered at the opening of the seals in Rev 5:9 that Jesus is worthy to do what must take place next. It is only He who can judge the earth. The sharp sword is a confirmation of all that He warned will take place. Dying for us showed that He did not come to condemn the world, but rather to save the world with His own shed blood. The judgment He wanted to save humankind from is now coming. Just as those who didn't listen in the days of Noah, so those who reject Jesus's words today will also not be safe.[a]

With many opposing Jesus, the armies of the beast and the kings of the earth are ready to do battle against Him. They think they have a chance! Clearly they don't. With swift action the beast and false prophet are captured without fuss and sent to the place of judgment. Remember the beast represented the kingdoms that oppose God and the false prophet stood for fake religious activity and demonic power. Those demonic forces that have used their power to influence humankind will be sent to the place assigned for them. Jesus is reclaiming the world which He had a key part in creating at the beginning of time.

What will become of the people who followed the beast and the false prophet? The One who is Faithful and True will judge them guilty. There is no one fairer to act as judge. Will actual vultures eat up their dead bodies? That sounds grim! It's picture language for total ruin; where no one is able to bury the bodies or scare away the birds, telling of complete judgment. Just as two gatherings were pictured earlier in Revelation, now we are shown two feasts. One is a joyful celebration of safety in the presence of God for those who have remained faithful to Jesus, described as a wedding banquet. The alternative is one of utter loss and desolation.

Jesus is both a lamb and lion. He surrendered himself to die, slaughtered as a helpless lamb. Yet He returns as a lion, on a mission to overcome the hold that evil has taken on our world.

Lord Jesus. King of all kings and Lord of all lords; Champion of heaven, I thank You for what You have won for me. As You surrendered Your life to save me, I surrender my life to follow and live for you. In Jesus' name.

THEN I SAW HEAVEN OPENED,
and behold, a white horse!
THE ONE SITTING ON IT
is called faithful
AND TRUE,
and in righteousness he
JUDGES AND MAKES WAR.

#Day42

FINAL DEFEAT
Revelation 20:1-10

If you were ever to take on a job as a youth worker, it'll not take long before you develop your very own super power. I'm sure you can picture the scene: the youth facilities are open and people are milling around. Some folks are throwing some shapes on the Just Dance game, whilst others are playing the sort of table tennis where the ball rarely makes contact with the table. Everything has a nice atmosphere about it. Time to relax? No; because it can happen at any moment. You'll be having a cool chat or about to score on FIFA, when suddenly you get a feeling that all is not as it should be. Like a sixth sense you'll know something is afoot. You don't know how you know, but you have to stop and go and investigate.

Then sure enough, after checking those rooms that are out of bounds, you find them. They're playing on the drummer's precious drum kit, eating stuff with mayonnaise that you can't believe is making such a mess and what's that smell? Has somebody lit up? You're glad you've found them before someone else! This is the not so fun part of being a youth worker: being the responsible one! With great skills of persuasion, you manage to get the group back to where they can hang out. Yet that sixth sense is still nagging you, "You know what'll happen when your back is turned!"

This is the kind of situation God is dealing with in the part we just read. We see Satan bound, thrown into a bottomless pit and prevented from direct contact. After he's released for a short time we find out what he's been prevented from doing. What does the devil immediately go and do? The very thing he's been kept from doing! He deceives the nations to gather for attack; so that they march as one to surround God's people, attempting to destroy every last one (v 8-9). We've already read about this moment in Revelation 12:7-17, where the woman representing Israel (and the community of God's people) gives birth to Jesus. Clearly the devil's intent from the moment Jesus is taken up into heaven is to completely annihilate those who follow the Lord. Therefore the devil is bound, stopped from attempting to do this through the means of mass deception.

Something else began after Jesus died, rose to life and was taken into heaven. The followers of Jesus who have died, share in what is referred to as "the first resurrection" (v5). As we speak, those killed for their witness of Jesus and all His followers who have died and *"not worshipped the beast"* (v4) are enjoying time with the Lord in heaven! They are particularly blessed! What about those who haven't followed Jesus? They remain in a sleep-like state until the Lord returns in judgment, *"the rest of the dead did not come to life until the thousand years were ended"* (v5).

So the thousand years covers the period of time between Jesus' return to heaven and His second coming. But hasn't it been more than a thousand years since Jesus ascended into heaven? We have to remember what we've learned about Revelation. Firstly, these visions were given to be read out to the early church. We can unlock Revelation's secrets by first understanding how it informed the early church. Secondly we've seen how numbers in Revelation are given a Biblical meaning, rather than for the statistical purposes of counting or measuring. We discovered that the number seven is given to represent the number of completeness with the seven lampstands meaning the whole of the church. Revelation also has meaning for us all! God didn't show John the four corners of the earth to make him think the earth was flat, but to relay the meaning of something that would impact the whole earth. The thousand years communicates to the early church a long period of time, where the timelessness of heaven and the chronology of earth are synced to meet at the return of the Lamb.

The picture language of Revelation makes it possible for us to visualise abstract concepts, yet it doesn't make these things any less real. There is a real heaven, where God's people are sharing in His Kingdom. There is a real authority given to us now to release this Kingdom on the earth here and now. There is a real devil at work, who is bound in his abilities and a time will come where this restriction is removed. The devil wants a battle of Armageddon, but we're told clearly that he will be totally destroyed!

175

Maybe you are worried about events that are happening in our world today? As children of God, Jesus does not want us to be fearful. He can do something about that. As a way of bringing them before God, you might like to write here some of the events that are making you feel fearful...

Take a look at Psalm 18 and begin to think around the words that you are reading that tell you about what God is like. Start to remind yourself that since God is with you, you will know all of the benefits that God brings. He wants to help you to see how He is working in your life. As you consider these things, draw a picture of yourself in the middle of the circle (it can be a stick person!).

#Day43

LIFE AND DEATH

Revelation 20:11-15

Imagine you've arranged to meet up with a friend whom you haven't seen for ages; and as you pass by a trendy coffee shop you stop for a drink. It doesn't take long before you end up deep in conversation, turning a morning coffee into an afternoon lunch. As you continue to chat for what seems like hours, you can't help but feel distracted by someone who is sitting at a nearby table. They seem to be taking an unusual interest in your stories and you feel they are being a little too nosey. So mid-conversation, you stop to address this person who is listening in on your private conversation, to ask if you can help them.

To your surprise they reply with an exotic French accent, apologising for their rude behaviour before explaining that they are a writer. They've been captivated by the stories of your adventures and would love to write about your life. The thought of this proposal sounds too exciting to dismiss, so you agree to take their number. As you talk further with the writer, you discover they want to know absolutely every experience of your life so far. This begins to bother you, because there are some parts of your life you'd rather forget. There are certainly things you don't want friends or relatives to find out! Even now you feel the embarrassment of mistakes you've made. There's still a sting of regret for the people you've hurt as well as shame about the stupid things you've done.

The part we read today reveals the reality of deeds recorded in heaven. Each one of us will face Jesus at His judgment seat. Everything that should be known will be known. The rich and important will have their turn alongside the poor and homeless. All will be judged on an equal basis. Here the end of time has come. At this moment the realms of earth and heaven pass away, as do death itself and the place of the dead. New things are coming, but first the present life must be concluded justly.

John witnesses a scene of books being opened, where our good thoughts, words and actions, as well as the bad will be accounted for. Yet this won't be a case of adding up good deeds versus bad and seeing which is greater. No. The key question that will require an answer is this: Who did we follow? Was it the Beast or was it the Lamb? To say we believed in Jesus won't be enough if we haven't then tried to put Him first in our lives. We can't answer this question by saying that we went to church every Sunday, that our parents are Christians, or that we've been baptised. Stepping from death to life begins with believing that Jesus is God's Son; but it also interacts with what He did as payment for our wrong doing. Being truly sorry for our wrongs must lead us to ask God to forgive us, and in turn be followed by a promise of allegiance to Jesus. It's a covenant promise; a best friends forever pact. Putting Him first, we commit to live His way, to discover who He is and what He wants. The books opened will justly provide this evidence of a life committed to Jesus, proving that a name has the right to be in the book of life. As above all other books, this is the one that counts. *"And if anyone's name was not found written in the book of life, he was thrown into the lake of fire"* (v15).

What then is the second death? Obviously the first death is the experience of a body which comes to an end and stops functioning. It's part of being human where we return to dust, just as Adam was created from the dust. The second death is also an end. It's what happens to those who have not given their allegiance to God through His Son Jesus Christ. After they give up their dead, Death and Hades are *"thrown into the lake of fire"* (v14). They will be destroyed, never to return, no longer to exist. Those that follow Death and Hades will also perish, no longer to exist. That will be the end. This is different from the harsher punishment that the devil rightly deserves, being *"tormented day and night forever and ever"* (v10).

The Bible tells us *"it is appointed for man to die once, and after that comes judgment"* (Hebrews 9:27). This is the moment where we'll each have to face the King of kings alone. We're not expected to have lived a perfect life. If that were the case, none of us would make it through. For those whose allegiance is with Jesus the Lamb who was slain, an eternity awaits; a place in glory, lit by the presence of Almighty God.

and i saw the dead,

GREAT AND SMALL,

standing before the throne,

AND BOOKS WERE OPENED.

then another

BOOK WAS OPENED,

which is the book of life.

GOD'S ULTIMATE PROMISE

Revelation 21:1-8

If you've ever climbed up a mountain (or a very large hill), you'll know how much hard work it is. It's something that you just can't do quickly. If you were to try, your legs would turn to jelly in less than a minute. Ending up in a quivering heap is always the result of such ambitions, rather than reaching the top any quicker. At this point children will pass by and stare as they make their way to the top! So it takes a steady pace, any things you carry will only get heavier, unless they are food and water which are fuel for the journey. Hiking to the top is also a challenge of mental strength; where every ridge brings the hope of reaching the final summit, only to disappoint at the sight of yet another upward trail.

Being a Christian can be a bit like this. When challenges come up against us the thought to stop the climb altogether can come at any time. It could be a moral challenge where a relationship is testing your obedience to Jesus or the influence of friends leading your life in a different direction. When God seems distant or you feel uninspired in prayer or Bible study, that can also feel like an uphill struggle. What we read about today is the view from the top of the mountain. This view will encourage you. It's the reward that awaits those who persevere! Much like the slice of heaven you get at the top of the mountain, you feel the thrill of having completed the climb and take in the beauty of God's creation.

Throughout the Bible and particularly the New Testament, we are given the most wonderful promise from God: eternal life. Now that evil has been dealt with, the new things are able to take place. Today we're given a glimpse of this promise. As the first heaven and earth pass away, there's no distance between humans and God anymore! We're told *"the sea was no more"* (v1). Is this the sea of glass that was the dividing point between heaven and earth? It has finally been removed! Now John sees heaven and earth being joined as he witnesses the people of God together, descending from heaven, having been made new (v2). With renewed bodies that are immortal, the ability to sin is now gone. *"Behold!"* God says (v3), announcing this new thing that He has done.

First God announces that His original intention for humankind has come to pass, *"and they will be his people, and God himself will be with them as their God"* (v3). Now the Lord and His people will live together for eternity. You might have experienced this, where you're hanging out with your friends at summer camp and you're having such a great time that you just don't want it to end. God's desire is to be with us like this and is described by the words *"dwelling place"* meaning "tent of God." Of course God is "omnipresent" which means He is already with us invisibly by the Holy Spirit. However, this describes to us how God will be with us both in Spirit and physical form.

This is a great moment of comfort as God recognises the hardships you and I have gone through for His name. It doesn't matter how old we are, we all need comforting when the tears fall. How tender is God's love for you and me? Here is a special message for the early church where God is showing that He has seen every tear of those who have lost family and friends through arrest and execution. These were things that were not meant to be a part of this earth. Now things are new.

John sees all of this as a past event; which is God's way of announcing the certainty of it taking place. Yet God is not satisfied to let even one person go uninvited. His offer of eternal life is for all who desire to know God. Just as we need water to maintain the balance of our bodies, so our soul needs the sustenance that comes from God. You can't climb a mountain without stopping for water! This life is not meant to be done without stopping to be refreshed by God. The Lord wants you and me to conquer this mountain, to endure to the end and be found faithful.

Father God! I want to recognise how thirsty my soul is! Help me not to ignore the signs of my spiritual need of You. I will stop trying to make it in my own power. Holy Spirit, increase my spiritual thirst! In Jesus' name.

behold the dwelling

PLACE OF GOD

is with man.

HE WILL DWELL

with them,

AND THEY WILL

be his people,

AND GOD

himself will be

WITH THEM AS THEIR GOD.

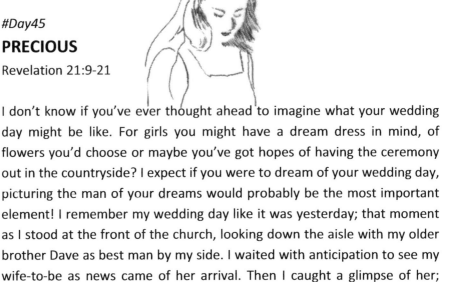

PRECIOUS

Revelation 21:9-21

I don't know if you've ever thought ahead to imagine what your wedding day might be like. For girls you might have a dream dress in mind, of flowers you'd choose or maybe you've got hopes of having the ceremony out in the countryside? I expect if you were to dream of your wedding day, picturing the man of your dreams would probably be the most important element! I remember my wedding day like it was yesterday; that moment as I stood at the front of the church, looking down the aisle with my older brother Dave as best man by my side. I waited with anticipation to see my wife-to-be as news came of her arrival. Then I caught a glimpse of her; seeing her took my breath away. She was stunning. There she was gliding up the aisle with the most enchanting smile. My heart skipped a beat as I watched my beloved walking towards me.

At that moment everything became a blur... no I'm not using a figure of speech, it all became a blur because a wee tear filled up my eye and my contact lens fell out onto the floor! Thankfully, I was prepared for this eventuality, having given Dave a spare lens in advance in case things got emotional. During the first song Dave got out a new lens and I saw her close up... laughing at me.

In the part we read today, God likens His people to a city and compares the moment we'll finally be with Him to a wedding day. *"Come, I will show you the bride, the wife of the Lamb"* (v9). John sees us, the Holy City descending from heaven, pictured like a bride walking down the aisle on her wedding day. As a bride groom gazes at his bride walking towards him, so God only has eyes for us. God is more interested in us than He is in the place where we'll be together. With hints of what heaven will be like, God reveals what we'll be like as His people. He's using picture language to tell us what this time will feel like when we begin eternity with Him in heaven.

In a moment we'll be changed and, like rare jewels, every person will shine with the glory of God. With our sins completely removed, we'll finally be the way God created us to be.

As we read about this city with walls and measurements, it's easy to get into Maths-mode to work out dimensions and convert them into metric. If we were to do that, the numbers we'd end up with would make no sense at all. Remember this city is a description of the whole of God's people. The number 12 represents those who are God's people; multiplied by 1000 which means a very large number.[a] There is space for us all! Why is this measured out? The shape of the city forms a cube (v16), the very same shape of the Most Holy Place that was found in the Old Testament house of God (1 Kings 6:20). This area was closed off by a thick veil to allow only special entry, as it was a place where God was physically present. The glory of God in the Most Holy Place was so pure and powerful that hardly anyone could go in. After Jesus died and rose again, God changed our access to Him by dwelling in our hearts by His Spirit. Even more change is to come in heaven where we'll have complete access to God in His glory and power.

Just as experiences together form friendships, so the shared history of God and His people is marked by twelve gates. These declare the "official" establishment of God with His people through twelve tribes. It's a heritage of memories made and of time shared that binds the Lord together with the people He loves. We as His church are included in this, linked with the apostles of Jesus who form the foundations to the New Testament church. The streets have a special type of gold (v21), one refined by a unique fire (Revelation 3:18). It's what we receive in exchange for our faith being proved true through the tough times we've endured. Jesus sees you and me as beautiful. As we submit our lives to Him, like precious jewels His light reflects through us shining out His glory for all to see.

Father God, You are my reward. I thank You for the promise of eternal life, where I will be close to You forever, safe in the security of Your presence. Thank You for the Holy Spirit, who reveals more of You to me. I thank You that even now, I can dwell with You and be close. In Jesus' name.

and the city
HAS NO NEED OF
sun or moon to
SHINE ON IT,
for the glory of
GOD GIVES IT LIGHT,
and its lamp is the lamb.

#Day46
TRANSFORMED
Revelation 21:19-27

From school prom nights to your wedding day; there comes a time in a person's life when you need to ditch that hoodie and those comfy jeans and make an effort to look your best. This is the kind of stuff those "makeover" TV shows are made of, where a nice hair style and carefully chosen wardrobe works wonders. "How can this be the same person?" we ask ourselves; as the TV show host announces that the newly found beauty will never be the same again.

It can be a similar transformation for the bride-to-be on her wedding day, with hair, make-up and nails all getting that five star beauty treatment. Essential to the look is a necklace of jewels that shines and a ring that sparkles in the light. The groom will hopefully take the time to visit the barbers for a styled look and a clean shave. Who knows? He might even make use of some skin care products? Yet no matter how much effort the man puts in, all eyes will be drawn to the bride. Everyone is ready for the moment she enters, to see the vision of beauty that she is transformed into for this unique moment. As the music begins, you can see folks trying to take a sneaky photo, whilst honouring the formality of the occasion.

The part we read today continues this vision of God's people in heaven being compared to both a city and a bride. Many people refer to the church as a building, when we know it's actually the people of God. A similar thing is going on here. Much like an ultimate makeover, we are going to be transformed into the likeness of God. In Revelation 4:3 the Lord has *"the appearance of jasper and carnelian."* Now God's people have *"radiance like a most rare jewel, like a jasper clear as crystal"* (v11). John confirms this in 1 John 3:2 *"but we know that when he appears we shall be like him."* Yet this isn't simply our outward appearance that will be transformed, there will also be a makeover of the heart.

We're given a description of the foundations of the walls being encrusted with twelve different types of jewels. Interestingly there were also twelve different precious stones attached to the breastplate of the High Priest's robe in the book of Exodus! Each stone was inscribed with a name of one of the twelve tribes. The idea was that the High Priest would enter The Most Holy Place carrying these stones close to his heart, showing how God valued His people (Exodus 28:21,29). As the High Priest performed his sacrifices to make amends for wrongdoing, the people of God were pardoned. The walls in Revelation are compared to The Most Holy Place with no need for the jewels to be brought in each time. Now they are permanently in God's Holy Place shining with the light of God.

What do we discover here? That a transformation has taken place! An inner transformation where we will permanently live by God's light, because we will continually shine with God's glory. This is something that words just cannot fully express!

So maybe you have noticed this about yourself... when you've been really connecting with God in prayer and worship or have been really inspired in Bible study, that you feel changed for the better. Somehow you have encountered God and that meeting with Him has made you more loving, full of peace or incredibly happy. When we get closer to God, we become the best version of ourselves as the Holy Spirit shines through all we say, think and do. The glory that the kings of the earth bring is the wonderful things that God has done through you and me as children of the King of Kings here on the earth (v24). Like a precious jewel God wants to shine through you and me today!

Father God. I know that from the moment I became Yours; You began a work in me, to change me as I experience Your glory in my life. I thank You that even now You are transforming me from one degree of glory to the next. I surrender my life for You to do this in me more and more. Holy Spirit, I welcome You to work afresh in my life. Come flood my soul with Your glory. In Jesus' name!

#Day47

THE TREE OF LIFE

Revelation 22:1-6

I'm assuming that having got this far through this book, that you don't mind doing a bit of reading! But have you ever got half-way through a book and decided to skip to the end, just to discover how it turns out? I have to admit, it's something I've done! I was reading The Lord of the Rings, and having made it to the third volume; I wanted to check that the ending was worth it!

Well you have made it to the final chapter of the book of Revelation and of the Bible itself! And yes, the ending is definitely worth it! What we read today describes the final destination for those who are "in Christ." Do you notice anything familiar about this place? It's not unlike the Garden of Eden, although there are some significant differences. John is seeing creation re-made with a second chance at the tree of life.

Interestingly to understand what happens at the end of the book, we need to check back with what took place right at the beginning! In the original Garden of Eden, the tree of life was freely available to eat from. However, this was not the tree that Adam and Eve found themselves gravitating towards. In Genesis 3 Eve engages in conversation with the devil who contradicts what God has told her. Both she and Adam are then faced with a choice. Do they obey God? Then they must reject the fruit from the tree of the knowledge of good and evil and instead eat from the one that brings life. Or do they believe the devil and eat from the tree which God said not to take? Something unseen is at stake. Whichever fruit they eat from, an irreversible change will result. Eating to gain knowledge of evil will acquire new abilities, but will also come at a huge price.

In many cultures a signature or a handshake is the act that makes an agreement binding. In the Garden of Eden, choosing which fruit to eat was enough to seal the deal. What results turns out to be a lot more than Adam and Eve bargained for. This wasn't a fact-based knowing of good and bad, as you might find in an encyclopaedia. Now they would actually experience bad things taking place, as evil seized its opportunity to lay a claim to the earth in a way which was legally binding. I'm sure you remember in Revelation 5:1-4 where there was the scroll containing the things which must take place that couldn't be opened. We saw a lamb appear looking like it had been killed, yet it was alive. We are told that this Lamb (Jesus) was the only one able to open it and break the curse.

In Revelation 22:3 we read *"No longer will there be anything accursed."* The word "accursed" comes from the Greek word *anathematizō* which means to bind or curse through an agreement. The curse of the Garden of Eden which came through an agreement will be completely removed. Nothing evil will be able to exist in heaven's space. Evil will be utterly overcome. There will be no more death, only life!

Now there's a second chance at the tree of life! In fact the other tree has been destroyed, since those in heaven have already made the decision to receive God's gift of life. What do we discover about this tree of life? It produces fruit that is only good. There are twelve kinds of fruit produced over the twelve months of the year. Twelve represents the number for God's people, showing that God will provide for all the needs of His people. With fresh fruit appearing each of the twelve months of the year, we're shown that His provision will be for all of time. It's quite a picture of peace, with a river flowing, rather than rumbles of thunder and peals of lightning coming from God's throne. Much of this language is meant to give us a feel for heaven, as well as to communicate meaning. Having God's name on our foreheads doesn't mean we'll all have an unusual tattoo, but rather it tells us that we'll know we belong to God. Not even night will be there to separate us from God as His brightness shines with love, power and glory.

Does this sound too good to be true? God assures us *"These words are trustworthy and true"* (v6). This is the intention of the book of Revelation, that we will know of all that is to come.

I remember the day when Jesus showed me that it was time to make my choice. As I sat in church, I knew all about God; but I had not made that decision to follow Jesus. All other decisions were irrelevant in comparison to this one. At that moment I decided to hand my life over to Jesus.

If you would like to do the same and take God up on His invitation to know Him, you can do this now by praying this prayer to Him. If you can speak (or whisper) it, all the better!

Thank You Jesus for Your invitation.

I come just as I am.

I know I have done many things wrong.

I thank You for dying on the cross for me.

Cleanse my life.

Set me free from the past.

I open the door of my life now.

I receive Your invitation.

I receive You into my life.

Come in by Your Holy Spirit.

Fill me with Your peace, Your presence, Your power.

Help me to build my life on You

Thank You Jesus for hearing my prayer.

You are now a follower of Jesus and part of God's family!!! Why not draw, write, doodle or scribble down anything that you want to say to God…

IDENTIFICATION

Revelation 22:7-21

Have you ever been close enough to a famous person to be able to get their autograph? There's something special about an autograph, because it links the item you have with the person who signed it. You have evidence to back up the story of your moment with a history maker! When I worked in London, there was a bookshop just down the road which often had book-signings, where authors would be available to sign your copy of their book. Often they would be happy to put in a personal message too. Occasionally sporting heroes would make an appearance to promote their autobiographies and the queue of waiting people would go through the entire shop and down the street.

I remember meeting the Arsenal Premier League Midfielder Paul Merson, a hero of my younger brother, Andy. It was a special moment when he wrote Andy a message in the front of the book. There was also the time I saw the legendary boxer Mohammad Ali visit that same bookshop. Such a large crowd turned up that the Police had to close the entire street!

As we read these last verses of Revelation, it's like Jesus is personally signing off on His book. The title of the book you've just finished reading is *"The revelation of Jesus Christ."* It's His words and His visions spoken to John with the help of His angels. I find it strange that for a second time John falls to worship at the feet of the angel. Yet overwhelmed by what he sees, John again has to be told not to. This moment does reveal something important to us. There's no doubt this angel is from God, since he refuses the attempt to worship him. Instead, he turns John's focus to God and God alone. A fallen angel would have responded very differently.

The words of Revelation are a reliable and true account. "Behold, I am coming soon" (v7) are the words of Jesus Himself, which mean that the events leading up to His return are at an advanced stage. Nothing can stop the return of Jesus, which can and will happen at any time. It will be sudden, but as we've seen in this book, we can't say we haven't been warned! We have God's words recorded for us; but we are also shown world-wide events in our time, demonstrating something is wrong with our world. Whether it's global warming, international terrorism, kingdoms falling, or deadly viruses, they each sound the alarm of the times that we are living in.

All of humanity is faced with a choice, *"Let the evildoer still do evil… and the righteous still do right"* (v11). Each one of us is responsible for our own actions. *"Blessed are those who wash their robes, so that they may have the right to the tree of life"* (v14), is a call out to you and me to take a stand and to identify with Jesus. It's so easy in this world to just go with the flow and end up living in a way that is no different from those who don't know Jesus. Yet we're handed an incredible opportunity from Jesus if we genuinely want to discover who God is, *"And let the one who is thirsty come"* (v17). This is both an invitation and a promise that God will reveal Himself to those who are looking for Him!

So it's not all doom and gloom! Jesus is returning! This is the heart cry of God's Spirit and of His people *"The Spirit and the bride say "Come""* (v17). Maybe you're not ready to think about heaven! Perhaps like me you have thought "I have my whole life ahead of me! There's stuff I want to do!" The more I discover about what this world is like and hear the stories of people's lives devastated by war, greed and selfishness, it makes me thank God for the hope of heaven. And I do begin to look forward to the time that is coming where the evil of this world will be utterly defeated, never to cause hurt or pain ever again. We might not like all that Revelation has to tell us about our world, but its words are true. They are signed off by the Lord Jesus himself. So we'd better not add to them or reject the bits we don't like. These are things that must take place, and then the end will come. We'll be with Jesus forevermore!

Lord Jesus. If this is the prayer of the Holy Spirit, then I will pray it too! May those who don't know you begin that search! Come Lord Jesus! Amen!

AND BEHOLD, I AM COMING SOON.

blessed is the one who keeps

THE WORDS OF THE PROPHECY OF THIS BOOK.

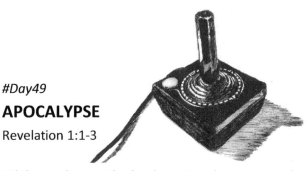

#Day49

APOCALYPSE

Revelation 1:1-3

Whilst working in the bank sorting cheques one day, I began talking with a friend called Matt about our experiences at Christmas. Matt recalled how (back in the 1980s) he was really hoping to get a brand new ZX Spectrum computer. On Christmas day he opened his presents to discover that he had been given exactly that!

So excitedly he took it upstairs to his room where his dad got it linked up to the TV and left him to it. This was going to be the best Christmas ever! In those days computer games took a considerable time to load. So to pass the time Matt went off for a drink. Deciding on a can of Coke, he took a sip at which point the game was ready to start. So Matt found a handy place for his drink next to the computer and reached for the game controller to begin playing. Unfortunately, as Matt reached for the joystick, he didn't notice the can of drink he'd just put down. Before he could do anything about it, the contents of his fizzy drink had spilled everywhere, all over his computer keyboard! Shocked and alarmed, Matt disconnected the computer and tried to blot the liquid from the keys. After reconnecting the computer back to the power and switching it on, all the computer could manage was to make a variety of fizzing noises. What a disaster!

If you were to ask someone what they thought the Biblical meaning of "apocalypse" was, I expect many would reply that it means disaster! "Apokalypsis" is the Greek word found in John's manuscript, which translated in to English is *"Revelation"* (v1). You might remember that we said early on how apocalypse actually means "unveiling." So rather than predicting the end of the world by a meteor strike, or a nuclear blast, this apocalypse unveils the purposes of the Lord which *"must soon take place"* (v1). These events are ordered by God to lead to the day when Jesus returns. Like lightning, Jesus will suddenly return in the sky where every eye will see Him. This is the apocalypse that God promises, rather than a catastrophic event that destroys the earth and every living thing. We're shown very clearly that God is in charge and that the unexpected global events of famine, war and hardship both alert and point us to Jesus' imminent return. Like a mother about to give birth, so the inhabitants of the earth will experience pain as a signpost to the times that we are living in. But why do we have to experience such difficulty? If all was well, would people ever be alerted to the unseen dangers ahead? The struggle of the process of evicting the devil from the earth is well underway and his destruction following judgment is in no doubt.

As God's people we are sealed and protected from anything that could remove us from the hands of God (Romans 8:38-39). Yet we aren't immune to the sufferings that come through persecution. This is something we need to learn. This is the very real background to the book of Revelation, where the followers of Jesus were arrested, imprisoned, tortured or killed for their faith. Just as Jesus suffered, so may we. When bad things happen, it doesn't mean that God has left us. When people give you grief for your faith in Jesus it is proof that you are truly His. A faith that is genuine will be tested. So don't give up! Stand firm! We're called to patiently endure and hold to the testimony of Jesus Christ.

Revelation helped those being ill-treated for the sake of Jesus. It showed them that suffering was not evidence for those who say there is no God. Rather, it's expected that we will be targeted, because the enemy knows his time is short (Revelation 12:12). As God reveals a fuller picture of what is to come, we understand more about the influence of the enemy on the earth; but also our trials are not the end! It appears the devil thinks there's a chance he can win, assembling an army to surround and eliminate God's people (Revelation 20:7-9). Yet the devil's end is certain. He will be *"thrown into the lake of fire and sulphur"* (v10).

In this life we will have trouble, but God has prepared such glory for those who remain faithful to Jesus! This is the life of faith. Trusting God in both the good times and the times of trouble will result in a crown that will last for eternity!

THE REVELATION
of Jesus Christ,
WHICH GOD GAVE
him to show
TO HIS SERVANTS
the things that must
SOON TAKE PLACE.
he made it known by
SENDING HIS ANGEL
to his servant John

ABOUT THIS BOOK

[a] https://www.zsl.org/london/coronavirus-safety-measures-at-london-zoo (see also "This Week" magazine, issue 236, 20th June 2020)

#Day7 TRUE VALUE

[a] Via Robert Young Pelton, THE WORLD'S MOST DANGEROUS PLACES published by Harper Resource. There is some discussion on the internet as to the behaviour and speed of anacondas! So please don't bet your life on the Peace Corps' advice on this one!

#Day17 PATIENT ENDURANCE

[a] "Vanya" by Myrna Grant Published by Charisma House

#Day19 NOTHING TO FEAR

[a] Some people read of four angels and four corners and think that these events must take place during seals one to four, as there are four horsemen. However, Revelation 7:1-3 only talks about harm to the land, sea and trees, and not the rise of empires and wars of the first two horsemen (Revelation 6:2-4). What the winds bring seems to be more consistent with the happenings of seal six. Also it would seem a strange place to refer back to seals one to four. The simplest explanation is that chapter 7 is a continuation of seal six opened in Revelation 6:12-17.

#Day 26 – SAVED

[a] The number of 1,260 days refers to the time period between Jesus' ascension, until His second coming. This is also referred to as 3½ years or "a time, times and half a time" as found in Daniel 12:7 (a year, two years and half a year). A prophetic year was considered to be 360 days. So rather than being something that measures time as we know it in seconds, minutes and hours, this refers to God's timing.

[b] We've already seen the relevance of the number two in the book of revelation, with the 24 elders being made up of two lots of twelve in Revelation 4:4. One twelve stood for the twelve tribes of Israel, reflecting the people of God before Christ and the other representing the twelve

disciples. Again in Revelation 7:4 we see the 144,000 made up of two lots, 12 tribes x 12 disciples which is then multiplied. With this in mind, the two witnesses appear to also represent this combination of the Old and New Testament witness through the ages.

#Day 29 – SIGNS

[a] Researchers (Frederick A. Larson) have identified a possible the date of 11th September 3BC to be the date that the star was first noticed eastward in the sky from Iraq. Because the stars and planets orbit in a clockwork-like movement, experts using computer software are able to reproduce exactly the movements of the stars in the sky even from 2000 years ago. Maybe you've been to a planetarium and seen this? Mary and Joseph would have travelled to Bethlehem in 2BC for the census, when Jesus was born. That's right Jesus was not born in 0BC! There isn't such a date!

Here's a sketch taken from an astronomy app that shows what the sky would have looked like the time the star appeared. The wise men were in the east (probably Babylon), looking eastward when they saw it. As the earth orbits, so the stars are seen gradually rising in the sky, going overhead until they set in the West, which is the direction the wise men travelled. The special brightness of the star they follow is thought to have been a combination of the brightness of two stars, possibly the planet Jupiter and the star Regulus (and later Jupiter and Venus). What we are looking at are constellations, which any astronomer would recognise. This is not astrology. (I'm not saying these stars had any influence on events, or provide any guidance). God did not create the stars to give us advice; but rather He gave us the Bible and the Holy Spirit to guide us! John simply says a sign appeared in heaven, going on to tell us what he saw in his vision. As you can see, the description of the scene from Revelation is very similar to what was displayed in the sky at the time of Jesus's birth!

#Day 30 – TARGETED
[a] Cornelius Tacitus "The Annals" Book XV Chapter 44

#Day34 – SOWING AND REAPING
[a] Passion iconography – J.H. Marrow p.80. Some stained glass windows picture Jesus being the first cluster of grapes to go through the winepress of God's judgment. Called the "Mystical Winepress" these can be found in Troyes Cathedral and at Saint-Étiene-du-Mont in Paris.

#Day41 – OVERCOMING EVIL
[a] Matthew 24:36-40 talks about one being taken and the other left. In the days of Noah many were suddenly swept away in judgment after they had rejected God's chance of rescue.

#Day45 – PRECIOUS
[a] Revelation 21:16 says, *"And he measured the city with his rod, 12,000 stadia."* It might appear differently in your version, but the original Greek text literally translates as "stadia twelve thousands."

A RECIPE FOR FAITH

Paul Martin has also written 40 day devotionals for young people.

A recipe for faith is a 40 day devotional for young people and teenagers. This book deals with issues of worry, anxiety and fear from the perspective of David found in Psalm 34. Could you imagine being on the run from the king and his army?! In your quest for refuge, you flee to the most unlikely place in a desperate attempt to find safety. You're afraid, very afraid. Once this fearful moment has passed, God speaks and you write this Psalm.

Psalm 34 will be an incredible encouragement to you as you find your way through the ups and downs of life. It's in the busyness of everyday life that God wants to talk to us: where we're battling fear or when life is stretching us beyond our ability to cope.

Over the page are the first few devotions from the book:

THE WHISPER OF FEAR

"David took these words to heart
and was very much afraid," (1 Samuel 21:10-15)

They say "desperate times call for desperate measures." Take a moment to imagine that you're a successful warrior. You're a fighter so outstanding that people have sung songs about you and the king together; but now you're out of favour. You've been sneaked out of the city and you're on the run. People are unaware that you are missing, so at least you have a head start.

In a short time you are sure to be pursued. Someone powerful is after you and if they catch up with you, you're doomed. This man was your friend, but now you are twice as much his enemy as you were his friend. Maybe you could escape from this one man; but there is an army ready at the king's command, sure to be despatched at any moment. These men will not give up until they have found you.

It appears there is nowhere to flee; nowhere to hide where they won't find you. So in desperation (maybe even as a stroke of genius), you go for safety in the one place where they are least likely to look for you. Unfortunately there's a small problem with this place you have stopped at; it just so happens to be the capital city of your actual enemies the Philistines. A dangerous place to find safety!

In a previous battle you killed their champion fighter (a history not easy to forget). Plenty of people will want their pound of flesh to avenge his death. So you try to hide your identity disguising yourself as a peasant. Yet those in charge have been alerted to your presence. Their servants are everywhere and in no time you are brought before the king.

You've come a long way from being a shepherd boy out in the country, facing off a giant when everyone else was too fearful to try. But now you have escaped with your life and very little else. Talk about going "from the frying pan into the fire!" So as you are brought to the king of the Philistines you are sure that he will satisfy himself by drawing his sword and killing the slayer of Goliath. This is probably not the time to mention that you know where the sword of Goliath is! Kings were known for their lack of patience as well as their ability to prove their authority with instant executions. The thought of what this king will do terrifies you.

We read the words *"David took these words to heart and was very much afraid..."* The servants of the king are quick to remind him of David's warrior status. "Pssst! Hasn't he killed loads of Philistine soldiers? Fathers, husbands and sons of ours who will never return to their families?" Instantly David feels vulnerable, unarmed and at the mercy of the king of his enemies. Fear takes the opportunity and whispers in his ear "You know what?? You're done for!" And in this moment of pressure David listens to the whispers, he believes the voice of fear. Panic seizes David and he loses sight of the truth that God has promised him a future!

It's after this moment of terror that David writes one of the most powerful Psalms in the Bible. It's powerful because it contains a way out from the negative place that fear can take in our lives. David found a place of freedom from anxiety through God's power and wrote about it. I believe that God wants to lead you into a place where you find yourself depending more and more on your Heavenly Father for all that you need, so that fear will find it hard to take hold of your heart.

As we begin this journey away from fear and towards faith, why not commit to pray this with me:

Father God. I need you. I understand the negative effect that some fears can have over my life. During the next few months please lead me to find the way out from the harmful fears that hold me down. I need You to lead me into a place where I will discover safety and freedom.

FEAR IN THE HEART

"David took these words to heart..."   (1 Samuel 21:10-15)

I wonder if ours is the generation that has written more words than any other in history? Think about it for a moment, we're always on our smartphones or tablets communicating to our friends, writing posts, comments or blogs. But with all this writing, comes the risk of being misunderstood. I'm sure you've had a text from someone and thought the person was being rude, just because it was written in a certain way. So helpfully, someone invented emojiis! A little smiley face, a sad face, winking face or even a love heart can fill in the emotional blanks that can be missed by the words we use to communicate.

We all know that a heart emoji communicates love or caring feelings and when the Bible talks about "the heart" it's describing more than just a feeling; it represents that deep part of us. It's where we decide things, it what moves us to cry or laugh, our motivations come from the heart and with it we can feel vulnerable or afraid. So what did it mean, *"David took these words to heart?"*

Remember we read yesterday about David's desperate attempt to escape from King Saul's imminent man hunt and how David ended up in Philistine territory? He's taken to Achish, king of the Philistines, whose servants bring up David's warrior exploits against these Philistines. They argue the point: "Can we trust David our enemy to live among us?"

David understands that if the answer to this question is "No," then there is no alternative but to kill him. The seriousness of his situation gives rise to fear in his heart. Who wouldn't be afraid at this most desperate situation? And with panic starting to surge within, David can see only the negative outcomes that fear has persuaded him are just a matter of time.

You know fear can actually be a positive thing. Fear can alert us to danger. It can stop us from walking too near a cliff edge, looking into the mouth of a crocodile, or swimming with hungry sharks. That is what fear is meant for, to help us to avoid danger.

But there are times when fear can be triggered in us when we perceive we're in danger even where there isn't any; our mind becomes anxious and the body physically reacts. Maybe we have an increased heart rate, we find breathing or swallowing more difficult and we might feel sweaty or cold. It's possible that taking on negative thoughts into our hearts can reduce our capacity to do things like being brave. Even just coping with normal situations can become more difficult. When fear starts to take control it can also affect our motivation as well as our abilities.

A person who takes to heart anxious thoughts will act differently. Have you ever worried about something and thought, "What if this happens??" Our mind starts to process worst-case scenarios and as a result our capacity to have a joyful life is reduced. Worry leads to anxiety and fear.

Now it's easy to say this, but actually David wasn't in as much danger as he feared. A while back (with God's help) he had defeated Goliath the giant using a sling and a stone! And there is another reason why David need not panic; the prophet Samuel had told David he would be king and God's promise to him had not yet been fulfilled! God gave David a way out, it wasn't pretty; but he lived to fight another day!

So I want to ask you this: who are you more ready to listen to when bad news hits? Do you fear the worst? Does panic try to seize you? Why not remind yourself that you are being looked after by a rescuer called Jesus, who wants you to trust Him to provide for your needs and a way through troubles? Don't give up and think that terrible things will happen. God has a way through for you. As you reflect on this, turn the page as there's a prayer space for you to hand over to God those things that worry you.

SPEAK LOUDER THAN YOUR FEARS

"I will bless the Lord at all times;
His praise shall continually be in my mouth."　　(Psalm 34:1)

I bought this really amazing speaker. You know the type. They connect to your smartphone or computer and are small enough to carry around, but loud enough to blast out any tune enabling you to hear every bit with absolute clarity. It's great for wall to wall sound in your bedroom. Trouble is though, when I try to recreate that sound in a medium sized or large meeting room, even with the volume up to full it sounds so much quieter. If you're on the other side of a room full of people you can't even make out the words. The boom of the volume is no longer attracting the attention of the people in the room next to me.

Worry can be a bit like the sound from that speaker. Imagine that your worries and fears are blasting out loads of negative noise into your mind. It can feel like that is all you can hear and it's tough to block out its effects. It begins to process around in your mind like a song on repeat.

But what if you were to take those same worries or fears into a bigger room? What if you took a step outside of your thinking and began to invite God into the situation and think about God, His greatness and His love for you? Suddenly the sounds of your fears are in a bigger space. You will notice that they are beginning to turn into wee background music that you can choose to ignore. Suddenly you feel strengthened, empowered, encouraged and faith starts to rise in your heart.

How is that possible? It's all about the heart. When we fill up our heart full of God, fear gets pushed out to the edges where it ceases to have that power and influence over us. You see the sort of fears that we are talking about can sometimes be thoughts put there by an enemy who wants to make us weak. At these times we need a spiritual strength to fight back that only God can give.

So our Psalm begins with the words *"I will bless the Lord at all times. His praise shall continually be in my mouth."* You know these two sentences actually say the same thing using different words. It's like God is turning up the volume on His speaker and saying "You need to hear this!! So I'm going to say it twice! Praise out loud is really important!!" Maybe you know that you can pray to God with your thoughts; He hears those as well as the ones we say out loud. But there is this added dynamic when we use our voice to talk to God. We hear what we are saying, God hears what we are saying (obviously) and our enemy hears what we are saying. When we have words of faith and speak them out loud something happens. The volume of our fears decreases as our minds enter into God's room, God's space.

Obviously you know it's not about the noise you use, but rather that you vocalise the truth about who God is. Not only does it put our situation into perspective, it also reminds us who God is. When we speak out truth, inside our heart the cogs of faith start to turn! Something happens and God the Holy Spirit speaks His inspired words into our heart, causing us to feel braver about the situation we are concerned about. We'll realise that God is working in our lives and guiding us through our difficulties and leading us to the solutions for our problems.

So speak louder than your fears! Say it out loud! Remind yourself who God is! Okay. You might be thinking, "Talk to myself?? That's crazy!" Well, it's not just yourself that you are talking to! The Bible talks about encouraging ourselves with God's words; and even in Lamentations 3:24 it says "I say to myself, "The Lord is my portion; therefore I will wait for Him" (NIV).

On the next page there's some space to do just this. Why not think through some of the words in the Bible about God and whatever inspires you, note it down and read it out loud! Declare the praises of God!

"for **He** is the

living God,

ENDURING FOREVER;

His kingdom shall never be destroyed,

and His **dominion**

shall be to the end.

He **delivers** and rescues;

He works **signs** and **wonders**

in **heaven** and on **earth**,"

Why not find a Psalm that declares the truth about God and write it out with your own style of writing? As you write, think about the words and what they tell you about God.

#Day4

DECLARING HIS PRAISES

"I will bless the Lord at all times;
His praise shall continually be in my mouth."   (Psalm 34:1)

Let's talk about habits; those things we do regularly, because we did them yesterday, the day before and the day before. You know... things like getting up on time for school. And you know; if you go to bed and get up at regular times, after a while you'll just wake up at the right time, because your body clock has got used to it. Developing habits like waking up at the same time each day without an alarm only happens because you've done it on purpose. Maybe you've had to remind yourself to do it to start with and after a few weeks you got used to it, so you don't need reminding now, because you've gotten into the habit of doing it. Stuff like eating an apple instead of a Mars bar, holding off spending your pocket money all at once or remembering to check your bag the night before you have sports at school. They are all habits we grow into.

I get up on a Saturday morning to go on a 5K run every week. This is the first time I've missed it in about 15 weeks and it feels so weird not doing it. It's a good habit that I've only got used to because I've done it continually week in week out. I know that when I go running next week my body won't freak out halfway round the course, because I'm used to it.

Can we look at the same verse we read yesterday? Is that okay? Yesterday we talked about speaking out the truth about God. Our fears shrink back as the truth about God is spoken and the lies of the enemy fade. The reason why our fears sometimes gain so much space in our minds is that some fears do actually alert us to real danger. Yet the problem is that a lot of our worries and fears that appear to be alerting us to danger are actually telling us lies. There is no danger. But when we feel we face uncertain or unknown situations, fear shouts at us with possible negative outcomes. We can end up believing these lies and get unnecessarily anxious. Therefore we need to identify the truth.

If you've ever had an argument with someone and discover they are telling lies, as soon as the truth is presented what happens to the lie? It disappears. People stop believing it. It has no power anymore.

This is why it is important to remind ourselves of the truth about God. When we discover who He is, we will come to realise His influence in our lives and how He will not let the lies of fear materialise. He will provide for you as you trust Him. But it is easy to forget what God is like. Especially as we hear so many things said about God that are not true!

So David, this man who temporarily forgot God and became so afraid in the presence of the king of the Philistines; what does he say is a good habit to have? *"at all times... continually"* to have God's praise in our mouths. By declaring God's praise on a regular basis, our minds are hearing it, the enemy is hearing it, God is hearing it and we are remembering it. And as we do this repeatedly our confidence will grow in God's ability to deal with the things that worry us. The enemy shrinks back, as his lie has no power when the truth about God is presented.

Listening to fear is a bad habit which needs to be broken. It is broken by taking on some good habits. Regular, ongoing praise will lead you to know God more and to discover so much of His goodness.

Shall we talk to God about all this?

Father God. I want to see You for who You are. Would You help me to develop the practice of declaring Your praises every day? Thank You that You are present with me now. Please reveal more of what You are like. Show me more of You I pray.

finding identity

Finding Identity is about helping the reader to answer the question "Who am I?" Finding identity encourages young people to view themselves from God's perspective as found in Psalm 139.

"Search me, God, and know my heart:"

Over the period of 40 days this book will help you to consider what you are like. Our ways, character, abilities and purpose all have a bearing on our identity, in the context of our relationship with God. Finding Identity will take you deeper into Psalm 139 and at the same time begin to inspire you about who you are and who you were made to be.

Over the page are the first few devotions from the book:

GOD'S SEARCHLIGHT

"O Lord, You have searched me and known me!"   (Psalm 139:1)

Imagine you were given the opportunity to choose a superpower; just one ability, anything at all. What would you go for? I know this might take some serious thought, so take your time! For instance, there are the well-known powers such as flying, crawling up walls, super strength, producing ice from your hands, invisibility, mind reading and those sorts of things. Then there are the more unusual ones, like teleporting, power absorption and shape shifting. So many super powers and each one is different!

I know this might sound super boring as he's one of the more underrated superheroes, but I'd like to be like Aquaman! Why? Just because I can't swim! Obviously they are not real, but all of these superheroes have one thing in common: their true identity is kept hidden from most people. I expect if you were to have a superpower, you would keep it a secret too. Why? I guess it would make you more vulnerable to your enemies and the fame would force you to lead a secret life anyway?

I know the superpower thing isn't real, but maybe there are times when we feel that people don't really know who we are. Perhaps you're thinking to yourself "I don't even know who I am either!" It can take time to understand what we are actually like, as there are so many influences around us trying to mould us into a particular shape. Therefore answering the question "Who am I?" can be a difficult one. Identity is more than just having a passport, being born in a certain location or supporting a particular football team. These can communicate something about us, but actually knowing who we are deep inside is altogether more tricky.

Have you ever wondered what God actually thinks about you? We read the words *"O Lord, You have searched me and known me."* Could it be that God actually knows us better than we know ourselves? The word for "searched" takes the idea of examining closely, where God searches our hearts and even knows the reasons why we do things. He goes that deep. So those things that lay hidden inside us, God knows about. You have talents that lay sleeping which are waiting to be discovered. Good character inside you that reflects God's heart of love, mercy and kindness also awaits the opportunity to be revealed; He sees it all.

For the next 40 days we're going on a journey of discovery; both discovering who we are, but also who God is and our relationship with Him. When God searches our hearts it's for a reason: so that He might draw us towards Him. As this happens He will naturally transform us. God works in us to change us, to strengthen our confidence and to stir a loving compassion in our hearts that causes us to become who He made us to be. He knows how to draw the best out of us.

So my question to you is this... will you let God in to search your heart? Think about that for a moment. God who is holy, loving and pure will see what you are like on the inside. He sees it anyway, but He really wants to invite you to see what He finds, so that together you and Him can become close. There will be some things that He wants to help you with, such as hurts that need healing and attitudes that He can shape. Yes it may be a little bit painful at times, yet He will only lead you through these in order to help you, to comfort you and to set you free. So don't hold back, you can trust God to work powerfully in your life and you will be better for it!

Can you commit to pray this with me? *Father God I don't want to hold anything back from You. Thank You that You are a good, loving and pure Father who wants the best for me. Come and do what You want to in my life. Examine my heart and show me what You find. Please shine Your light on the dark places of my heart that I keep hidden. I thank You that Your love for me is not dependant on my heart, but rather on Your loving kindness. Please change what needs changing, show me what I'm good at and lead me to know what You want for my life. In Jesus' name!*

FINDING POTENTIAL

"O Lord, You have searched me and known me!"   (Psalm 139:1)

One of the interesting things I remember learning from my school days was in my Physics class on the subject of energy. There are different types of energy that an object will generate depending on what's happening to it. So if you are heating a pan, that object will begin to possess thermal energy. When you pick up that pan, that movement produces kinetic energy. If you had the know-how, you could build a wind turbine to convert the kinetic (movement) energy of the wind into electrical energy. All very interesting, but there is one type of energy that has always intrigued me: potential energy. Say I had a cup of water and I placed it on the middle of a table, it would probably not have much potential energy. Nothing much can happen to it there.

However if I were to place that cup of water on the edge of a table or even on someone's head, suddenly it has a lot more potential! If I were to tell that person a well-timed joke, the kinetic movement of their body as they laughed uncontrollably at my very funny joke would convert that into umm... well I only got a C in Physics, so we'll probably leave it there!

What exactly is God looking for when it says *"You have searched me and known me"*? Doesn't God know everything? So why does He need to search for it? I believe that one of the things He is looking for inside of us is potential. Potential is something that each one of us has which relates to the possibilities ahead of us, who we might be, or what we might achieve. It's there already stored up and it's waiting to be unleashed.

Maybe you're an artist and He sees what beautiful designs you can create, a mathematician and He is going to develop your mind for problem solving. Perhaps He sees a kindness in you that He delights to see you express? Maybe you are a deep thinker that can communicate complex ideas in a way that anyone can understand. Perhaps you are sporty and are born to win! Potential. Things that have not yet taken place, a history that has not yet been written. Does God search our abilities and see if we have the character to handle it? We're all a work in progress! But it's not just your role in life that God is interested in. As I said yesterday, He is interested in us because He wants to draw us toward Him.

God searches us to discover if there is the potential that we will get to know Him better. He is motivated by love. He's already thinking about you. Is there a potential in your heart to move towards Jesus? Imagine a school friend that you didn't know too well asked you out on a date. They'd be asking because they were motivated by love and interested if you like them. A boyfriend or girlfriend relationship is a closer bond than two people who just know each other. They want to spend more time with you, to talk and be together; when you are apart, you're thinking of each other. There's a potential relationship between you and God, where He has already seen you, loved you and wants to be close.

How then do I discover my potential? It's really important to say that our potential finds its best fulfilment when it's a part of God's plan for our lives. This is a journey of discovery that begins with an open heart to God, asking "God what do you want for my life?" He wants to reveal this to you along the way; and at the right time, God will add his kinetic energy bringing to life your potential. Often we don't know what we're made of, which is just as well that God does know. As you spend time with God, He will often hint at the things that you will do in the future and the talents that you have that are currently undiscovered. I've always loved drawing, but it was only when I was forced to pick up a paintbrush for GCSE art that I discovered I was a really good painter! Sometimes God causes circumstances that we don't expect in order that we can find out things about ourselves that we didn't know, but He knew all along!

Over the page is a prayer space to begin to discover the potential that God has stored up for you. Why not take some time to think it over with God?

FALSELY ACCUSED

"O Lord, You have searched me and known me!"   (Psalm 139:1)

Have you ever been punished for a crime you didn't commit? Maybe you feel there's a group of people who have the wrong idea about you? Perhaps you've experienced a situation where you just happened to be in the wrong place at the wrong time, with the wrong people? And now you've been associated with a deed you had nothing to do with. You're believed to be guilty even though you didn't do it. Oh the injustice!!

I remember an incident happening to me at school that went like this... I was minding my own business when two of my friends came running round the corner of the school building. I ran up to them and noticing they were out of breath, wondered what was going on. It was then that the headmistress came out of the building and she was raging! Next thing I know we were all getting a telling off by the headmistress, before she dished out our punishment. The following half hour was spent with each of us standing in silence in the assembly hall until lunch time was over! The exact details of what happened are a little sketchy as this happened over thirty five years ago, but I'm sure I was innocent!!

If my headmistress had known me a bit better, she would have discovered that I was actually a really well behaved young lad who avoided any kind of naughtiness at all costs. Sometimes people who don't know us well label us, or associate us with things that are not a true reflection of who we are. It doesn't seem fair and we just wish someone would set the record straight!

There are others who compare us to people or things that we would rather they didn't. I remember being called the name of a character on the TV and I hated it. I was nothing like that person! The trouble is we can sometimes feel others will link us to those we're being compared to and inside we're crying out saying "I'm innocent of these accusations! I'm not what you think I am."

So far we've said about this verse that God really knows us, our secret identity (if you like) and that God sees our potential, the person you and I can be. But there's something else that God wants you to know. He wants to reassure you that He cannot misunderstand you. He's not blindsided by people's efforts to define you, their careless words or ignorance. So if you're feeling misunderstood, just because people don't get you, God has searched you, He knows the truth. Nothing is hidden from Him.

As he writes Psalm 139 it's like the writer is saying "These people are accusing me of things I haven't done! But God you know me! You can even read my mind, so You know for sure what the truth is!" We are going to discover that even if you don't know God yet, you and He have a history. Isn't it amazing that He gets us? We can come to Him and immediately He is up to speed with who we are. How reassuring that there is someone who can set the record straight!

Maybe you're concerned about the false things people have said about you. God doesn't see you that way. You can walk tall, even when people lie about you. You can be secure in the knowledge that God defends those who honour Him with their lives; and He always looks out for His children. People can falsely accuse us, or put us into a box; but they can't take away the truth of who we really are. God sees who you are; both the good and the not so good. Whatever He sees, He invites us to come close to Him. You can be yourself with God, since He knows it anyway. You can talk normally and honestly, aware that you can't shock God!

Let's come to God then and ask Him to show you how He really sees you. *Father God. Thank You that You sent Jesus to bring me close to You. I want to know what You see in me. Help me to see beyond the labels and lies that people use to describe me. You really know me! Please reveal to me what You love about me. In Jesus' name! (Have a look over the page!)*

#Day 4

CLOSE BY

"You know when I sit and when I rise."   (Psalm 139:2)

Here's a riddle for you:

> Every day I appear, I'll sit at your feet.
> All day I follow, in cold or in heat.
> I'm as big as you are, but I don't weigh a thing.
> Move fast or slow I'll promise to cling.
> What am I?

I'll tell you in a moment! I want you to think of a person that you would love to spend the whole day with. Imagine you had "access all areas" to someone famous that you've always wanted to meet! You can learn a lot about a person if you just followed them around all day. If you stuck to them like glue, you'd discover how busy they were, the places they went to, who their friends were, what interested them on the TV, the things they valued, what they laughed at, as well as what they liked to snack on during the day! If you did this regularly, over time you'd begin to feel a part of that person's life.

Want to know the answer to the riddle? I'm sure you've guessed that it is a shadow! A bit like a shadow God is following our ways, always with us, closer that we think, even closer than your breath and He knows every detail. In our sitting down to rest and our rising to get something done, He knows it.

But why is God so close? What is He so interested in? Some people think wrongly of God that He is there to check up on us, like a strict school teacher, waiting for us to do wrong so He can add it to a list in His book. Let me tell you that is not why He is close by! Motivated by love, God is interested in the details of our lives. He sees the things that cause us pain, the challenges we face and the struggles of our lives and wants us to know that He knows about them too.

Maybe you've been practising a particular dance routine that you are struggling to get right for a performance; what if God were to tell you that He loved seeing you dance today and that you are really gifted at it. How would that make you feel? Maybe you would feel encouraged to not give up but to see this as part of who God has made you to be. Or perhaps you're wondering if you should still go to the youth group as you feel that no one notices you? What if God were to say that you are actually a key part of that group and things really aren't as good when you're not there.

Sometimes we don't always see ourselves in the right light. We put down our abilities and think we're not so good. Of course you might not be the finished product or at the level that you want to be yet, but God is with you in the process saying, "This is part of My plan for your life. Keep it up!" Or there may be times when you feel you don't contribute much when you're out with the group; maybe you've been labelled the quiet one as you are a bit shy. God is there too, and doesn't leave you (just like your shadow doesn't!). He wants you to see that He has noticed great things about you, things that He doesn't want you to give up on.

It is out of love that God takes a close interest in you and me. He really notices and cares about you! Psalm 56:8 says *"You have taken account of my wanderings; put my tears in your bottle"* which describes how tenderly God loves you. He feels the pain that we feel, and sees the times we are moved to tears, in heartbreak, sadness or pain. It registers with God who is so much closer than we think. Maybe this is a good moment to just stop and be aware of how close He is.

Lord Jesus. I thank You that You are my friend and that You are for me. I believe that You are alive and with me here now. Please make me aware of how close You are to me as I spend some time thinking about You...

Like or follow us on

facebook

...to hear about previews, freebies and new publications from the Inspire series.

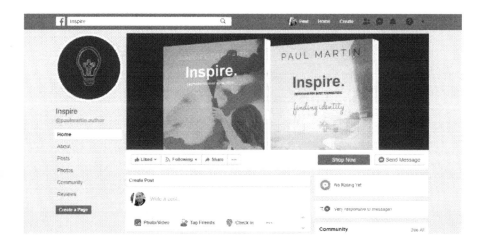

INSPIRE – A resource for busy youth workers - VOLUMES 1&2

This discussional resource is written for all those involved in youth ministry. With over 60 Bible interactive study sessions in each volume it moves chronologically through the Old and New Testament. Volume 1 tackles the big stories of the Old Testament like Noah's Ark, as well ones that may be less familiar to young people such as Job, Hagar and Eliezer.

Volume 2 continues where volume 1 left off, completing the Old Testament stories before moving on to the New. This resource is ideal for those with limited preparation time, yet want to take young people deeper into God's word and understand its applications in a more meaningful way.

Visit our website:

www.inspiredevotions.com

Amy Walters

Christian Graphic Design Artist
Logos, Print Design, Social Media Design

www.amywaltersdesign.co.uk
info@amywaltersdesign.co.uk

Printed in Poland
by Amazon Fulfillment
Poland Sp. z o.o., Wrocław

65166651R00132